Michele C. Moore

Michele C. Moore

Hungry Neighbors

hunger & hope in Northern New England

Michele C. Moore

Michele C. Moore

Michele C. Moore

Disclaimer: All of the profiles of people in this book are basically true, but I've changed the names (except where stated) and some of the details of food recipients to protect their privacy. The names of programs, directors, board members and volunteers are unchanged.

Michele C. Moore

CONTENTS

Michele C. Moore

PART TWO

ACKNOWLEDGMENTS

Many people have contributed to this book. First of all, I must thank the directors and staff of all of the food programs with whom I talked and/or visited. Many of you are named in the book and you all have given me invaluable help. Without your compassionate work, many Americans would starve.

Thank you to the recipients of food aid who courageously shared your stories with me. You are helping others to learn.

Thank you to my husband Chris, who happily drove me over New England roads in all weather and who took the photos that illustrate these pages. We had fun doing our research and met many wonderful, giving people.

Thank you to Martin, my writer son, the best editor and critic I know. He can see exactly what can make a piece of writing better and express this in clear, but encouraging words. And to Anshika, his wife, our daughter, who has formatted the book far better than I could ever do.

Thanks to Susan Hansmeier, Mary Anne Johnson and Jessica Hutchins for asking the needed questions.

And thanks to you, the reader; it is my hope that you will spread the message.

Michele C. Moore

PART ONE

Michele C. Moore

"There is hunger everywhere, fear, cold poverty, like old, used, damp clothing, like old, withered, fallen faces."

J. M. G. Le Clezio

Introduction

This book grew initially from my interest in the sustainability of our local food pantry program. My many years as a practicing physician had acquainted me with the local need for emergency food, but I didn't really know the extent of the need or who were the clients. Certainly I heard friends characterize the clients as "welfare moms" and people with substance abuse problems, but I didn't really know anything about those hungry people who weren't my patients. As a bookaholic, I first looked for books to inform me about food programs and food insecurity in New England, or more generally, in rural America; when I didn't find any, I then decided that I should visit programs and perhaps write a book. I found a wealth of statistics in the Feeding America annual reports to the states, the US Census data, the United States Department of Agriculture programs and their websites, Forbes magazine, and in the writings of a number of economists. These are necessary, but dry and faceless facts. I needed to put a face on hunger and hear the stories of real people.

To this end, my husband and I began a yearlong pursuit of food programs. We visited most of the counties in New Hampshire, as well as programs in Maine and Vermont. Together we listened to many stories and heard the reality of hunger – from young mothers to classily dressed young working people to the disabled and the elderly. If we began with any stereotypes, they were soon blown away.

One of the first things we learned was the difference between food pantries (called grocery programs by the USDA) and food banks. A food pantry is a program that distributes food directly to the households who will consume the food. These are usually community-based and have only local impact. Food banks are larger distribution hubs, like a grocery wholesaler, and supply groceries to the various local food pantries and feeding (communal meals) programs. Each state has one (sometimes more) food bank and these distribute to most of the more localized programs in each state. Most of the food banks are affiliated with Feeding America, a national food distribution, policy making, and advocacy group that is essentially a coop of food banks. Feeding America enables food banks to further the economy of scale so that food banks can have access to groceries from other areas in the country at (usually) better than market prices. All of these organizations are voluntary non-profit organizations.

We also learned that many programs operate in a sort of isolation, in that the directors and volunteers don't know what other programs are doing or how other programs meet challenges. For this reason, I needed to include information about the rules and structures of the various programs so those intimately involved can compare and be inspired. These programs, from tiny to larger, are not static. They are organically evolving in the quest to constantly provide better services for their clients. Because of this, the stories I've written about the individual programs should be viewed as candid photos of the time at which they were interviewed: many of the programs will have made changes or instituted new methods or policies by the time this book is published. This is particularly true for the Fall Mountain Food Pantry and Friendly Meals.

In our search for the faces of hunger in our region, I learned that many prefer that hunger not have a face. This was true for the gentleman who signed up to volunteer at the Community Kitchen in Keene, NH, only to quit after his first afternoon of filling grocery bags for the pantry clients. He spotted his neighbor in line to pick up food and was shocked. Theirs is a solidly middle class neighborhood, so how and why could someone from these circumstances find himself in a bread line? And the man has family. Our friend, the volunteer, was overwhelmed by his emotional response to seeing his neighbor. It frightened him. It is equally true for recipients of food aid. As Lisa Pitcher, director of Our Place, in Bellows Falls, VT, said, "We often see people choose to go to the next-closest food pantry to where they live. If they have transportation." She explained that people are embarrassed and humiliated to be seen as needy in their own community, by people they know, and that they will often travel to the next closest food pantry to fill their needs. So I learned that the hungry bear the stigma of their misfortune, instead of having the onus fall on our wealthy society.

As I traveled northern New England, I saw that huge gaps exist between what is available and what is accessible, between what's on paper and what goes on the table, between our ideas of ourselves and the reality. Most frighteningly, I learned of the bleak future facing many of our seniors as the baby boomers retire – it was like Scrooge's vision of Christmas future – and the concomitant cuts to food programs in the federal and state budgets, year after year after year. Although many programs go along day by day, week by week, averting crises but not solving problems, some people and programs and the whole state of Vermont are thinking proactively of ways to put our enormous collective resources into service to our people. I learned of gleaning – what I thought of as a medieval term – and the farm/food program collaboration to save food from waste and instead put it in the bellies of hungry people.

After spending six months on visits to various locations, it was clear that there is a certain sameness, dictated by the requirements of the USDA and the food banks, to the operations of the various programs. The differences were in the stories of the people.

Another impression that formed midway through these visits and persists today is that the programs that have at least one paid staff person are better able to innovate and plan for the future. Although local donors often remark that they don't want their donations going to the overhead of paid staff, the reality is that most of the programs without paid staff are not able to add programs, such as meals or budget help or cooking classes, because the time and energy of the volunteers is tied up in maintaining the existing pantry program from day to day, week to week and to constant fund raising. There are exceptions and they seem to be church-based programs (e.g. St. Thomas More in Durham and Harvest Christian Church in Berlin). I think this is because some of the work of the food program is done by church personnel – notably the financial record keeping and fund raising – and the security of being part of a larger organization relieves some of the burden usually born by a willing few. We forget that the willing few in each community are themselves subject to aging, illness and infirmity.

What started as curiosity turned into an obsession as I realized that we are becoming less as a society by allowing the erosion of the potential of almost twenty percent of our children through high calorie malnutrition and outright hunger, by not ensuring to the best of our abilities that our seniors do not starve, by complacency as we see the plight of children in Angola and do not see our own faces in that mirror. There are relatively simple ways to ensure food for all, but we need the will and this will not come if we are not informed.

Client contemplating his choice of produce from the "free table."

Fall Mountain Food Shelf

The Fall Mountain Food Self serves the area in which I live. To be precise, it serves five communities in the northern tip of Cheshire County, and southern Sullivan County, NH. Much of this is a "food desert" and these communities are mostly poor.

Town	Ranking/240 Towns	Per Capita Income
Acworth	207	~ $24,000
Alstead	177	~ $26,000
Charlestown	211	~ $23,000
Langdon	112	~ $32,000
Walpole	155	~ $28,000

Like many living in Alstead, I had taken the food shelf for granted – oh sure, I wrote my annual or semi-annual check to support its work, but had no real knowledge of how it operated or what its future might be. Again, like many in town, I'd been aware that it is an organization that depends heavily on one person and that that person is getting on in years, so it was a shock to realize that Mary Lou, the director, had been unwell. I began to worry about the viability of the food program if and ultimately, when Mary Lou was no longer able to head it.

The critical moment for me came at the Memorial Day service on the town green, when I encountered Mary Lou Huffling after not seeing her for many months. Over the next month, I thought hard about how to proceed. I cornered a selectman at the Farmers' Market and asked him what he knew about the food pantry and its future viability; he knew as little as I. I combed the Internet and book stores for any information about rural food pantries, especially in New England and found only the occasional old newspaper puff piece encouraging donations. Eventually, I decided to ask Mary Lou Huffling for an interview, telling her that I was researching a premise for another book and would write an article about Fall Mountain Food Shelf for the local paper. However, I really wasn't sure what I wanted to ask her; it was a bit bald and tactless to say, "what will happen to the food pantry when you are no longer able to run it?" So, prior to talking with her, I turned to technology and searched for information about hunger and non-profits, food banks and food pantries, building a pyramid of crusts and rinds.

A good source of information is the United States Department of Agriculture, aka USDA, and there I found that the statistics are versed in terms of "food insecurity" and that this is defined as limited access to adequate food because of lack of money or other resources. Knowing this gave me access to the statistics: I learned that in our state of New Hampshire, one in nine individuals is "food insecure," including forty-two thousand one hundred seventy-two children. As if this is not bad enough, New Hampshire is actually one of the better states: it ranks number nine among the states, meaning fewer of our families go to bed at night with a cold stone in their bellies. Vermont ranks seventeenth and Maine, thirty-second.

Another resource was a website that gave clear instructions for starting a food pantry posted by Feeding America West Michigan and another by the National Council of Nonprofits. I was delighted to find this. This was the source of many of the specific questions that I determined to ask about the local food pantry and any subsequent food programs that I visited. Among these questions were: is it incorporated as a 501(c)(3) charity; does it have an active and involved board; are there written by-laws and a mission statement; is there a written transition plan or a system of cross-training board members; are the accounts audited and are electronic databases kept? This was a list of important questions impacting the sustainability of an organization - questions that I would not have thought of on my own, but to it I added more questions. Several of my friends had grumbled that "anyone can go and take food" and that "is there any means testing" and "people come over from Vermont …it's not just local people" So these became questions to be asked. I also wanted to know the demographics of the population served in order that I could put faces to these numbers. I had read that many seniors were in need and had the image of our neighbor Ruth, now deceased, who had huddled in one heated room in her old family home, eating tea and toast, as all old ladies are supposed to do, getting two hot meals per week at the senior meals, and coming to us for Thanksgiving. How many Ruths are out there?

The Fall Mountain Food Shelf is currently housed in a frame building in Langdon, NH. The building was home to a plumbing business and has housed a physical therapy office, as well as other small businesses. It sits on NH State Highway 12A and is remote from the villages it serves. In fact, Fall Mountain Food Shelf serves five villages: Langdon, Alstead, Acworth, Charlestown and North Walpole and bridges two counties: Sullivan and Cheshire. When I arrived on a Saturday morning in July 2014, there were five cars parked outside the food shelf entrance. I noticed that two of them wore Vermont plates. Detractors of the food shelf might be chagrined to note that there were no Beemers, but instead a miscellany of pickups and older vehicles.

Mary Lou, the director, was not there, so a volunteer offered to pass on the message that I had been trying to reach her. I looked around and saw that two women were pushing battered grocery carts around an island of canned goods and boxed foods. At that point, Mary Lou arrived and explained that she had set the food display up in such a way that people could "shop" and choose their own grocery items. She then showed me the refrigerator that contained dairy products and eggs and a freezer with frozen meats and poultry. She said, "Each week, I try to give them eggs and some meat – not a lot, because it's expensive – and some milk, if I have it." She chose a tentative time to come to my house during the following week to go over my questions.

Over a cup of tea, we talked about the history of the food shelf and how it grew. The Fall Mountain Food Shelf was born around 1978, after gestating in a Well Child clinic in Charlestown, NH. The Well Child clinic was run by the visiting nurses of what is now Home Health Care and Community Services and aside from the nurses and the doctors who gave their time (I was one of the clinic doctors from 1982-1984), the clinic was run by community volunteers. These were mostly mothers of young children who attended the clinic. The volunteers doing intake realized that there were families in need of food and other daily necessities and Home Health Care asked the women to start a food closet. A nucleus of concerned volunteers – Helen Bascom, Mary Lou Huffling, Gail Fairbanks and Mary Lou Pelton – began to stock a free-standing metal cabinet with emergency canned food and dry goods. There was space for little more than this in the couple of rooms allotted to the Well Child clinic in the old frame community building. The women also began to canvas for donations both of money and non-perishables. Access to the food was constrained by the hours of the clinic and soon it became obvious that more room and availability was needed for the food shelf. At that point, the Episcopal Church in Charlestown offered space to host the food shelf and it moved to the basement social hall of St. Luke's Church.

In the early eighties, unemployment rose and so did gas prices, and the need for another site was realized: the Alstead church donated the use of a hallway off its fellowship hall and the operation in Charlestown was moved to the old Town Hall (which accommodated refrigerators). The Alstead arrangement worked for several years until increased use and the decision to provide fresh foods – eggs, milk, etc. – necessitated the purchase of refrigerators and freezers and therefore a need for more space. The answer to this need was the relocation of the food shelf to space generously donated by Helen Bascomb in her home, where it stayed until Alstead's sleepy Cold River tried to absorb thirteen inches of rain in twenty-four hours in October of 2005. Its failure devastated this small town, with flood waters rushing cars and trees over the railings of the bridge in the middle of town.

Many lives were affected by the flood (characterized by state engineers as a five-hundred-year flood), and many needed emergency food. Fortunately, there was an outpouring of donations – both money and food – from many communities and organizations in both NH and VT. After transient housing in a space donated by the Masonic Temple in Langdon during the immediate aftermath of the flood, the food shelf moved to the Baker Building, originally the home of a plumbing business, in Langdon, where they remain today. (The Charlestown branch is housed on Woodrise Rd in a rented building donated by the Town of Charlestown.) The use of this building, plus heat and utilities, is donated by the Town of Langdon. Similarly, the Town of Alstead has donated the use of a building on Bragg Lane, in Alstead, NH, for the preparation of the Friendly Meals, as well as the use of the Town Hall/Fire Station for the serving of the Friendly Meals. The Friendly Meals are community meals for seniors. Neither of these sites (Baker Building or Bragg Lane) is secure because they are subject to vote and renewal by the Town Boards at short intervals (one to three years.) Mary Lou Huffling stated that it is her dream that the Food Shelf has a permanent home. Her concerns are justified because the food shelf will have to move by January 2017 – the building has been sold and the new owners have plans that do not include a resident food program.

Fall Mountain Food Shelf has an informal organizational structure; it does have a board of directors, who are self-elected and are drawn from the more committed friends of the food shelf.. Being committed to the mission of the food shelf is the only criterion for board membership; there are seven members of the board, ranging in age from fiftyish to ninety-one. No terms of office are set – board members serve "until they get tired or resign." There are no regularly scheduled board meetings: "we see each other all the time and just come to consensus." There is no attempt to recruit board members with particular skills that would be helpful to the organization, e.g. legal, fundraising, etc. One board member has grant-writing skills and she has written successful grant applications for the food shelf. Mary Lou Huffling is the director, elected by the board sometime around 1982. She has been the only director and has no term limit. She points to her tenure as evidence that there has been no need for a transition plan. There is a mission statement, but no operating plan, by-laws or standing committees. A transition plan had not been discussed at the time of these interviews.

Fall Mountain Food Shelf is not a 501(c)(3) non-profit. An application has never been made. The Friendly Meals is incorporated as a 501(c)(3) – the legal work was donated and filed more than twenty years ago. Donations for the Food Shelf can be tax-deductible if they are made to The Friendly Meals, which now acts as the Food Shelf's fiscal umbrella. You may well wonder what the connection is between the Friendly Meals and the Food Shelf. They are staffed completely by volunteer labor – no one is paid - with some cross-over between the two groups of volunteers. According to Mary Lou, the meals are prepared and transported to the Alstead Town Hall where they are served from a building donated by the Town of Alstead. Meals are also transported to shut-ins (Meals on Wheels). The food for the meals is kept separately from that of the Food Shelf.(This status has changed: The Fall Mountain Friendly Meals is now the fiscal agent for Fall Mountain Food Shelf, providing the umbrella of its 501(c)(3) status and the structure imposed by such incorporation.)

Mary Lou notes that there has been a change in the composition, as well as the numbers, of families served over the past thirty-five years. Originally the Food Shelf served around thirty to forty families per month, and these families represented all age groups. Now the approximately fifty volunteers serve twelve hundred to thirteen hundred families per month, with a growing number of elders in this number. This represents a change in attitudes and in the ability of families, as times have become leaner and meaner, to take care of their elders.

New families are asked to complete the USDA application for government surplus food, which is used for many programs, e.g. WIC, food stamps, etc. This is the only time that the recipients are screened. Thereafter, when arriving to "shop," they are asked to sign in with their name, address, new or returning status, number in family, number over age fifty-nine and number under age nineteen. These are entered in a database (electronic) and a monthly report is generated for the USDA and a quarterly report for the NH Food Bank. A report of numbers of town families utilizing the Food Shelf also goes to each town each year for the respective annual Town Report. New volunteers at the Food Shelf are oriented to observe confidentiality of the participants, be welcoming and non-judgmental. They do not sign a confidentiality agreement.

Donors are people like you and me, churches, businesses, service organizations such as the Rotary or Lions, schools (several school clubs and organizations, like InterAct, Jr. ROTC and the National Honor Society help with the holiday food boxes) and a couple of family foundations. The Towns of Walpole and Acworth make a yearly monetary donation toward the purchase of food. One family foundation gives a matching grant to donations raised in the spring; another will donate twenty thousand dollars, if a similar amount is donated by the community in the autumn. The agriculture department at Fall Mountain High School donates plants for gardens. Ninety percent of the food is purchased, primarily from NH Food Bank and various supermarket chains (Walmart, Discount Food Warehouse, and Cheesco) who give the food shelf a discounted price. Occasionally, a grocery store will donate excess items and there is a history of greater food donation in the past. Local farms and gardening families donate some fresh fruits and vegetables during harvest. (Signs are posted at the relevant post offices, saying "Grow a row for the Food Shelf!") Donors of food and the volunteers at the food shelf have liability coverage through the NH Good Samaritan Law. This does not cover general liability for the physical facilities and in the absence of such insurance coverage by the Food Shelf, the liability probably falls on the town that owns the building.

I asked Mary Lou how this food shelf differs from others in the state and she replied that at most food shelves, recipients are given a pre-packed box of food, containing a balanced assortment of items. At the Fall Mountain Food Shelf, people enter a building that is configured like a store, with shelves of items arranged in logical order. There are three shopping carts, each fitted with a banana box. People shop the shelves for the items that they need and that their families like to eat and they fill their banana box. In addition, each family is given a dozen eggs and a small amount of meat. The food shelf can no longer afford to give milk, except when they are occasionally able to purchase shelf-stable milk from the USDA and/or NH Food Bank. The families may come to 'shop' as they need.

In answer to my question about a point of weakness, Mary Lou said that it is hard to know if there will be enough volunteers on a given day – sometimes there are too few and other times, a lot show up. She also said, ". . . and you never know how many families will come on a given day. It always works out and if we need help, there are always clients who come in and are willing to pitch in and help – always. Also, the rising cost of food impacts the food shelf just as it does the families that need the services and it is heart-breaking to have to cut back. It is imperative to have balanced food choices available, but some foods are becoming difficult to impossible to afford (milk, meat)." No databases are kept to detail or organize the flow of volunteers, food or monies. The paper listing of client flow is the only database and it is later entered digitally for the purpose of reporting to the USDA and the NH Food Bank plus the breakdown by towns for the towns' annual reports.

In July 2015, this food pantry was one of forty in New Hampshire chosen by Well Sense, a Medicaid managed-care organization, for delivery of five hundred pre-packed bags of food to be delivered by the Mobile Pantry through the New Hampshire Food Bank. Many of the communities of Northern Cheshire County and southern Sullivan County, NH are considered food deserts, with a high percentage of people living at or below poverty level and with poor access to full-service grocery stores. Transportation is also a critical issue here, as there is no public transportation at all.

The Fall Mountain Food Shelf is also a resource for borrowing durable medical equipment that people have donated after their need has passed. This is a great help to families caring for elderly or ill relatives.

If additional need is noted, clients are referred to the appropriate government agencies, e.g. for fuel assistance, food stamps, prescription drug assistance.

Mary Lou said "I think that if the rest of the world was as kind to needy families as in our area, we'd have no problem with hunger. .. the clients leave the food shelf feeling cared for." I requested meetings with board members and volunteers. I wasn't refused, but somehow they never materialized, even though I know one of the board members quite well. She (the board member) commented that she had no idea about some of the things I was asking, e.g., transition planning.

My curiosity was piqued: I wanted to find out more about hunger in northern New England, so I set out to visit at least ten programs in the three northern New England states. I was especially interested in who are the hungry, why, and what the future looks like. We still don't know what will become of the Fall Mountain Food Shelf, although the great need should trigger a community action should it threaten to fail.

It's Personal

Perhaps visiting food programs and spending hours researching hunger seems a strange avocation for a retired physician. However, the passion that I've brought to this investigation has its roots in my own experience of hunger and my fear of its specter looming over my own old age. The latter is what makes many not want to look at what is happening and makes them want to avoid the realization of their own vulnerability.

When I was in my twenties, soon after college, I moved from my small bucolic village in far northern New York to New York City. I was in search of a job that wasn't teaching high school science – I had tried this for one year and failed to meet a high standard.

In New York, I found a research job and a studio apartment in Greenwich Village. My salary was just adequate to cover my fixed expenses, plus food and transportation and I was comfortable for the first six months. Then, like many foolish young people, I thought I could do more . . . specifically, loan money to a friend. Worse yet, I took out a personal loan at the bank and loaned the whole amount to a friend. Of course, you know the story: the friend squandered the money that was to help him get established in a new job, and I was left holding the bag. Unlike many young people today who simply do not have the opportunities to earn an adequate salary, this was a situation entirely of my own making.

I paid back the loan, but it meant that for the next year, I had to choose daily between skipping a meal or using the subway to and from work. Most of the time, I skipped the meal. I also stopped drinking milk altogether, deciding that that was an economy that wouldn't harm me. After six months, I received a small raise at work and was again able to just manage my paltry finances. As was usual then, I received regular merit and cost-of-living raises and within a year, my situation was comfortable, if not affluent.

The second time that I was hungry was in medical school. I studied medicine in the sixties, when women weren't very welcome in the professions in this country, so I studied in Dublin, Ireland. The Irish commitment to educating women doctors was admirable, but as a student in Ireland, I was not allowed to work. And as an American studying abroad, no American scholarships were available to me, except for the Federally-subsidized loans. The result of this was that my fifteen hundred dollar yearly loan paid my tuition and I lived on less than one thousand dollars per year from my savings. By lived, I mean paid rent, food, heat and hot water, any medical costs, and clothing. It was less costly in Ireland, but this was still a stretch.

How did I manage? Like many people today, I skimped on food and I walked instead of using public transportation. My daily menu was boring: one slice of brown bread with a thin slice of cheese and a cup of tea for breakfast, one whole meal bun, a cup of yoghurt with a packet of peanuts poured into it, an orange and a cup of tea for lunch, and for dinner, I alternated one soft-boiled egg and a piece of brown bread or a roll with the same bread or roll and one-half can of tuna. And of course, a cup of tea. One year, I was on a brown rice kick and that replaced the evening bread. Good friends were my salvation; at least once monthly someone would invite me for a meal and during the times that I had to be resident in one of the hospitals, meals were included.

My plight was never as dire as many of the people whom I've met on this quest to learn about hunger in northern New England today – I had no dependents to feed and worry about. And I was confident that if I could just stick it out, my future would be brighter. Nevertheless, once you've been hungry, it colors your view of people and your community.

Through my forty plus years of medical practice, I've known many hungry people of all ages, including children whose only meal each day was the school lunch and seniors who literally only ate saltines and hot water because that was all they could afford. Early on, when I met children who were malnourished, I blamed the parents and was quite judgmental – even reporting one young woman for neglecting her child. This shames me now, because I learned that these parents were starving themselves in order to provide what they could for their children. Yes, there was a handful who had other issues, like alcoholism, but most of the parents were trying very hard.

And I didn't know that social security benefits were not enough to ensure a dignified life for elders or that some, especially older women, received too little to even live. I learned this lesson from an elderly patient – when I first met her, she was working for the Green Thumb program – a program that employed seniors and allowed them to earn a small stipend for community service jobs. I knew this woman for many years as she aged and developed minor health problems. Minor, but she was unable to buy the medications to treat them. For a time, the drug company agreed to supply her (after she and I filled out reams of paperwork documenting her need) but finally, that source of help also dried up. Her world narrowed to the walls of her subsidized housing apartment and she became more and more frail. This woman was a giving and vital part of our community until poverty essentially walled her off and robbed her of sustenance and dignity.

Today, as I sit at my computer after visiting all these programs and talking with all these people, I am anxious about the plight of my peers. I am in my seventies and know that I am not immune to the illnesses or injuries that drive so many of us to bankruptcy and insolvency. Like many other seniors, my husband and I have been frugal almost to the point of penuriousness so that we could look forward to living with dignity in our own home for the later years of our life. But, as you'll realize when you read Ellen's story, this may not be enough. We still grow much of our own food, but we may still find ourselves hungry when illness or simply the frailty of age deprives us of this. Like many, we have good adult children, but they are also not immune to the exigencies of life and may not be able to help us. I fear the specter of cold and hungry years at the end of my life and of life shortened by malnutrition. It is hard to avoid bitterness when one sees one's friends – like Lulu – in these straightened circumstances, knowing how much these friends have given to their communities. Surely it is time for us as a nation to stand up and take care of our own?

The Problem

Hunger is an American problem. In the US, in 2014, fourteen percent of households were food-insecure. Food insecurity is the term used by the US Department of Agriculture and other agencies instead of hunger. It seems that food insecurity is easier to quantify than hunger. Household food insecurity is defined as not having enough food to meet the needs of the members of a household because of lack of money, opportunity, or some other barrier (e.g. illness or frailty).

Hunger affects every county in the US, but the problem is greatest in the South, with a rate of hunger exceeding the national average of fourteen percent, e.g. Mississippi (22%), Arkansas (19.9%), and Louisiana (17.6%). In comparison, the northern New England states are doing very well, but Maine is also above the national average. In Maine, sixteen point two percent experience hunger.

Many of us have not realized that hunger is a problem in the United States; many others think that hunger is an inner-city or Third World problem. It is surprising to find out that fourteen percent of all Americans have too little to eat. This translates to forty-eight point one million people, including fifteen point three million children, for whom hunger is a daily reality. This is one in five American children. Map the Meal Gap is an online tool posted by Feeding America and it allows you to look at hunger statistics specific to your own county – or anywhere else in the US.

Hunger in the United States is a rural problem and there are challenges specific to being poor in a rural area. They are:

- Employment is more concentrated in low-wage industries and many rural workers earn minimum wage or less;

- Unemployment and underemployment are greater;

- Education levels are lower;

- Work-support services, such as flexible and affordable child care and public transportation, are less available;

- The rural marketplace offers less access to communication and transportation networks; and

- Offers companies less access to activities that encourage administration, research and development, thereby attracting fewer new industries.

Our rural areas produce the bulk of the food that feeds our nation, but many rural poor have limited access to food. These people live in food deserts. A food desert is an area (technically, a census tract – or census unit) in which twenty percent of the population is identified as poor and in which access to a grocery store or another healthy, affordable retail grocery outlet is limited by distance – one mile in an urban area, ten miles in a rural area. Many of our rural areas are food deserts. When I was working on a remote reservation in New Mexico, it pained me that the nearest convenience store was thirty miles away and the nearest grocery store sixty miles away. The fact that the trucks hauling wonderful produce from southern Arizona to all parts of the US were passing us by a mere hour away on I-40 was insult piled on injury. Perhaps this is an extreme example, but all you have to be is ten miles away from a grocery store, especially if you are without transportation, you are ill or elderly or you can't buy gas for the car that sits in your yard.

So far, our "solution" to the problem of hunger has been voluntary – that is, through the charitable efforts of Americans. We are a generous people, but strangely, we often view need on the part of our own as somehow lacking in virtue. We often adhere to the old bootstrap mentality that here in America everyone can succeed. Certainly that has been our heritage, but it is no longer true. As you read the stories of people who volunteered to share a peek at their lives, you will see that many of us are slipping from middle-class to a more marginal existence. In fact, for many, middle-class is simply a remaining set of cultural values and aspirations that have become unattainable. Inequality is killing our society.

At the local level, food aid is dispensed through a variety of food shelves or pantries, churches, emergency boxes from town resources and individual acts of charity. Mostly, these food programs are members of the respective state's food bank. Food banks are essentially distribution centers at state level and at least one exists in every state. They also set standards of safety and cleanliness for all of the food programs buying food from them. Yes, buying. Some sell food at a set per pound cost, some act as discount warehouses. In turn, they usually buy discounted food from Feeding America or grocery wholesalers, such as the Independent Grocers Alliance. They also distribute donated food to the various food programs – this donated food is termed "free food". All food programs participating with the food banks also have to adhere to the US Department of Agriculture rules for distributing government surplus food and the food banks are depots for distribution of this food. In the chapter on food banks, you will see that they also run a number of other programs that benefit recipients.

Feeding America is a hub for all of the food banks and serves them by distributing donated and discounted foods and by doing research, marketing and outreach for the nation's food banks. Each food bank pays an annual membership fee. The amount of discounted and free food that a particular food bank can access from Feeding America is allocated according to population served by that food bank. This turns out to be a disadvantage for the less-populated rural states and inadvertently favors states with large urban populations. As I've mentioned, all of these programs are voluntary and depend on donated dollars; they also compete with each other for the same dollars. Each holiday season, I receive appeals from Feeding America, the New Hampshire Food Bank and our local food pantry. Like most of us, especially those of us on a fixed income, I have to make choices and either I give a pittance to each organization or I pick one to give to more generously.

There are many government programs, as you will read in the separate chapter on these. Many, such as the School Lunch and Breakfast programs, benefit children or children and mothers (WIC). There are also a number of programs for elders, such as the communal meals programs and Meals on Wheels. The Supplemental Nutrition Assistance Program is utilized by all ages and is probably the most successful governmental program in that it helps both the recipients and the general economy.

You will also become aware, as I did, that there is a coming crisis in senior hunger. It makes sense: the seniors and baby boomers who are currently becoming seniors were the hardest hit by the Great Recession and they don't have time to recover financially before retirement. Actually, for many, retirement has become a myth once heard about at their mother's knee – many have to continue dragging their ailing and infirm bodies to work every day. And the most marginal are also the most infirm. Many had begun work with the promise of pensions – these disappeared. This is a problem nationwide and will have a very deleterious effect on our economy as a whole, as well as on families.

Hunger is not remote; it exists in your neighborhood and mine and may be the lot of any one of us. I have the hope and belief that we are good enough as a people to find compassionate and dignified solutions to this problem and to become a stronger and more cohesive society in the doing of it. This is the reason for this book.

Colleen

Colleen lives in one of our small New Hampshire towns, sleepy little places that close down at six in the evening. In Colleen's town, there is a convenience store and a gas station, but no other businesses. No public transportation links the town with anywhere else.

Colleen is in her mid-twenties and has a degree as a physical therapy assistant, but she's been unable to find a job in her exact field. Instead, she has found a job as a nursing aide – a forty-hour/week job that pays eight dollars and twenty-five cents per hour. She does have benefits, but forty dollars per week comes out of her paycheck toward these benefits. The job is in the small city twenty-four miles away from her home so she has to commute. Last year, when Colleen first got her job, she considered moving closer, but the rent for her current studio apartment costs seven hundred eighty dollars per month, and includes heat. In the larger community, it would be over eight hundred dollars, plus heat and utilities. She realized that she couldn't afford to move. (Rental housing in New Hampshire averages one dollar, twelve cents per square foot and keeps rising. This is at least partly because of the high real estate taxes in New Hampshire, but rents are also high in Vermont and Maine.)

Here is Colleen's monthly budget:

Income – payroll deductions:

Monthly gross pay	$1430
Federal Withholding	- $147.33
Social Security tax	-$88.66
Medicare tax	-$20.76
Benefits	-$173.34
Net Monthly Income	**$999.91**

Fixed Expenses:

Rent	$780
Commuting (work only)	+$110.07
Utilities	+$75
Telephone	+$10
Total Monthly Expenditure	**$975.07**

Colleen has only $24.84 left each month with which to buy food, any medication co-pays, dental work, and gas for such things as grocery shopping or going to a food pantry. Note that there is nothing left for any of the pleasures of life that most take for granted in our society. As a frugal New Englander, Colleen has been trained by her parents to not sign for cable TV or any entertainment for which she cannot pay. Basic cable TV costs around fifty dollars per month in this area.

Colleen's life is blighted by the constant worry that she'll have no food and that there is no way that she can afford a well-balanced diet. She skips meals and has her intake down to one meal daily now and often goes the whole weekend without eating. Work offers a little respite from hunger, simply because her co-workers often offer her a portion of their meal or bring baked goods to share. Besides feeling hungry much of the time, Colleen is humiliated because she's gained about fifteen pounds since leaving college. She spends her food dollars on the most filling and cheapest food that she can find – and a treat for her is from the dollar menu at McDonalds, which is near her work.

My first thought on talking with Colleen was "why doesn't she apply for food stamps?" And then I did the math. To receive food stamps, your income has to meet certain guidelines: it needs to be one hundred thirty percent of the poverty level or less. The poverty level for one person is eleven thousand six hundred seventy dollars per year. Colleen's gross income is seventeen thousand one hundred sixty dollars per year. To be eligible for food stamps, she would have to earn less than fifteen thousand one hundred seventy-one dollars per year. So Colleen's only hope of filling her belly is private charity, aka voluntary food programs, and this is the scenario for most of the 'working poor.'

To the casual eye, many working poor do not look poor. In fact, Colleen often wears clothes with very good brand labels in them – she's quite expert at picking over the used clothing on offer at the thrift store next to the food pantry to which she goes once monthly. Since the "purchase price" is by donation, Colleen owns an Anne Klein suit, designer jeans and three cashmere sweaters. But no food in her fridge.

Colleen still considers herself relatively lucky. "I have a full-time job and am proud of that. I contribute to society. So far, I've managed to stay out of debt – which I could never repay – and I've not gotten sick. I'm young, so I keep thinking that things will change. If the minimum wage is increased, my pay will also go up. Or maybe a job in my field will open up – I keep applying. Although, I've learned that the pay isn't great there either. Anyway, every time I go to the food pantry, I see people who are worse off – families with little kids and the old people, who shouldn't have to be hungry at this time of their lives. Yes, I'm not so bad off." In fact, in New Hampshire and Vermont, fifty-seven percent of the households using food pantries have incomes below the federal poverty level. (See appendix A) In Maine, it's fifty-six percent.

Colleen is an optimist. Her cup is always half-full. However, high calorie malnutrition is beginning to take its toll on Colleen, young as she is. She has borderline high blood pressure and is pre-diabetic. The only lifestyle change that she is able to implement is adding exercise to her day – she now goes out for a walk on her lunch break (it also helps her to not think about food.) Her diet is mostly canned and boxed, with a half-dozen eggs and a little meat from the food pantry. Sometimes, mostly in the summer, the food pantry has fresh fruits and vegetables available and to Colleen, this is like being given precious jewels. "I'm lucky because I do have a fridge and stove. Some of the people I've met at the pantry have nothing to cook on." (The statistics show that two percent of these people have no access to cooking.) Although all of the pantry directors and volunteers whom I've met have the common goal of providing healthy foods, they are still constrained by available donated money and goods and clients end up with a high proportion of carbohydrates like pasta, baked beans, canned corn, etc. It fills the belly, lards the limbs and falls short of a balanced diet.

It is a shame that Colleen isn't eligible for food stamps. The Supplemental Nutrition Assistance Program (SNAP) is the program administering food stamps. It is a federal program and interestingly, has been touted by advocates, policy wonks and economists as one that actually works. Not only does it efficiently increase access to healthy food on the part of the SNAP client, it also puts more money back into the economy than it costs. Studies vary a little in how much is generated, but the average is around one dollar seventy-three cents for every SNAP dollar spent. You can imagine how this works: Colleen (or Joe or Anne) spends her food stamp dollars at the local grocery store, paying the market price for her groceries. The store makes its profit on this and pays its employees. The store also uses a part of it for advertising and to pay the wholesalers. And so, the dollar put in grows to one hundred seventy-three percent positive impact on the economy.

Three Food Banks

A food bank is a non-profit charitable organization that distributes food (groceries) to those in need. In the United States, most, if not all, food banks operate as warehouses supplying food to a network of food pantries and meal programs that serve hungry people directly. The first food bank in the US is St. Mary's Food Bank Alliance in Phoenix, AZ. St Mary's was founded in 1967 by John van Hengel through his parish church, St Mary's Basilica. Van Hengel became aware of the need for a distribution center for food for the needy while he was a volunteer at St Vincent de Paul (a Catholic charity) serving meals to the hungry.

After visiting the local food pantry, it seemed logical to visit the NH Food Bank. Since food banks service the various grocery programs (pantries/shelves) in the particular state, the directors would have an overview of hunger in the particular state – NH in this instance. It was from Bruce Wilson, for example, that I learned that NH has three impoverished areas: the north (Coos County), the southwest (western Cheshire and southern Sullivan Counties) and the seacoast area (eastern Rockingham and southern Strafford Counties). Many of us who live in NH are only aware of the poverty of Coos County.

The food banks are the hubs of the food distribution network serving the hungry. Since St Mary's Food Bank Alliance began in 1967 food banks have proliferated and now each state in the contiguous US has at least one such organization.

In 1984, Monsignor John Quinn of the Manchester (NH) Diocese of the Roman

Catholic Church decided that he must feed the hungry . . . that it was the right and Christian thing to do. In his capacity as head of Catholic Charities, he founded the New Hampshire Food Bank, which still operates under the non-profit status of Catholic Charities of the Diocese of Manchester. The Mission of the New Hampshire Food Bank "is to feed hungry people by soliciting and effectively distributing grocery products and perishable foods, and offering innovative programs through a statewide network of approved agencies; by advocating for systemic change; and by educating the public about the nature of, and solutions to problems of hunger in New Hampshire." It belongs to the Feeding America network of Food Banks and other programs across the country. Although New Hampshire Food Bank is an agency of Catholic Charities, it is non-denominational in its operations.

Vermont and Maine also have a Food Bank. The Vermont Foodbank is headquartered in Barre, Vermont, with distribution centers in Brattleboro, Rutland and Wolcott. Good Shepherd Food Bank is in Auburn, Maine and also has warehouses in Brewer and Biddeford in order to serve the different regions of Maine. Like the New Hampshire Food Bank, these act as a hub for the networks of food programs in their respective states. They coordinate with Feeding America and its nationwide network of resources and research capabilities. They also are non-denominational and non-discriminatory. The food banks in these three northern New England states are not aligned with any political party and receive bi-partisan support in their respective states. None of them receives any government funding.

Good Shepherd Food Bank of Maine was started by a small prayer group, meeting at the home of JoAnn and Ray Pike. In 1981, the Pikes read an article about the Harvesters Food Bank in Kansas City. They had already been aware of and deplored the waste of food that they saw around them and they contacted the Food Bank group in Kansas City for more information. This was the impulse that grew into Good Shepherd Food Bank, which today partners with over six hundred food programs to serve the hungry of Maine. The Vermont Foodbank was founded in 1983 by Joseph Kiefer and Joseph Gainza, working with a group of around eight people who were involved with a community action program. Community Action Programs were instituted through the 1964 Economic Opportunity Act which was an integral part of the "War on Poverty." Guess what – we lost that war and it seems as though we've quietly turned our official back on it, but it did spur action such as that of Kiefer and Gainza.

Bruce N. Wilson, the Director of Operations of the New Hampshire Food Bank gave my husband and me a guided tour of the food bank's permanent home – a fifty-seven thousand square foot building on East Industrial Drive in Manchester, NH. Coincidentally, the original home in which the food bank opened on World Food Day in1984, was a six hundred square foot garage on the same street. In that first year, two hundred fifty thousand pounds of food was distributed to the hungry in New Hampshire. (In 2014, the amount was over eleven million.) The Food Bank moved into its permanent home – purchased and renovated for the purpose – in 2010. It is a marvel of efficiency: the flow of people and food is directed by the layout of the building in one-way traffic to minimize the possibility of accidents and to maximize the circulation of groceries to storage and to distribution. All electrical systems, refrigeration, heating, etc. are computerized and monitored through a central control room, to maximize energy efficiency and guard against disruption in refrigeration, leading to perishable food spoilage. The electrical supply is backed up by a four hundred sixty KW generator, so passing hurricanes and blizzards don't disrupt the system or endanger the foods. The subdued lighting and scintillating circuit board in the control room make you feel as though you are in a space ship.

The warehouse storage area has the capacity to stock around twenty-one hundred pallets of boxed groceries. Because of the constant movement of groceries into and out of the facility, this area is seldom filled to capacity, but having a large storage space enables the food bank to take advantage of bulk purchasing of the groceries that it buys and thereby stretches donor dollars. Wilson has brought his expertise in for-profit business management to the food bank and runs a very lean and efficient operation. This efficiency extends to the fiscal management: ninety-six and one-half percent of the budget is allocated to operations and only three and one-half percent to administration.

Another efficiency instituted at the Food Bank is real time ordering: this means that the inventory of the warehouse is continuously updated online and that programs as remote as those in Coos County have the same access to immediate ordering as do programs in Manchester and its neighboring communities. This is not only efficient, it also ensures fairness. For example, if a shipment of fresh apples is donated, it won't be all gone before Vickie in Berlin or Phoebe in Keene knows about it. Vermont and Maine also have real time ordering – it is an equitable system.(Obviously, programs with hired staff who are able to monitor the inventories online have an edge over those completely volunteer programs whose staff have primary obligations to their wage jobs.)

About fifteen percent of the groceries obtained are bought by the Food Bank, using donated money, and most of these purchases are from Allied Independent Grocers, who have the policy of giving to the food bank a very generous dollar rate per pound of food. Wilson explained that Allied Independent Grocers are, collectively and individually, committed to being responsible members of their local communities. Currently, the price to the various food programs for groceries from the food bank is eighteen cents per pound. Also, Wilson explained that the grocery industry has a very tight profit margin and of course, they want no waste. To be able to sell groceries that are still edible but near the sell-buy date is only good business.

Unfortunately for the hungry, grocery chains are constantly working on and improving their ratio of wastage to supply, so there is less for the food programs. Shaw's supermarkets now flatly state that they have no waste. This greater efficiency adds up to more profit for a grocery store, but less food donated to the hungry. In 2012, the Vermont legislature passed the universal recycling law (Act 148). This law requires any business generating one hundred four or more tons per year of food scraps to recycle this food. A hierarchy has been set up, with all better quality food (unused, unadulterated) going to feeding programs for people. The next best quality food (scraps from plates, etc.) is to be donated for animal feed and the food scraps not suitable for ingestion (partially decayed, dirty, etc.) will be composted.

All food bought or donated to all three food banks (NH, VT and Good Shepherd, ME) is subject to rigorous food safety inspection and the twenty-seven full and part-time paid employees of the NH Food Bank are required to be trained in food safety. The NH Food Bank is certified by two external agencies, the American Institute of Baking, International, and Feeding America, whose standards are set by the USDA. The New Hampshire Food Bank also requires that each of its member agencies (your local food pantry) have at least one responsible person trained in food safety and that that person be responsible for the safety of the food distributed via that particular program to individual families. This is important because the food bank supplies half of the food available from the local programs in New Hampshire.

The NH Food Bank distributes food to the hungry ten percent of New Hampshire people through four hundred seven partner agencies. It has bipartisan support from politicians in the state, while remaining politically unaligned and receives no government monies. All monies come from private citizens, businesses and grants. The same applies to the Vermont and Maine food banks.

All of the finances of the organizations are kept on electronic databases that have backup systems in place and the finances are transparent and audited.

New Hampshire Food Bank has a partnership relationship with the four hundred seven agencies (food pantries, community meals programs, etc) that it serves. In order to benefit from this relationship with the Food Bank, the partner agencies must have non-profit status, either as 501(c)(3) organizations or under the umbrella of another incorporated charity (as we saw with the Fall Mountain Food Shelf). They must also be oriented to the rules and responsibilities of being affiliates and take a four hour food safety training. An Agency Relations team from the Food Bank visits each partner food program once yearly to check up on required documentation, the cleanliness and safety of the physical facility and food handling and to get feedback from the particular program. The Vermont Foodbank has two hundred twenty-five participating food programs to which it supplies groceries, training and advocacy and Good Shepherd in Maine serves over six hundred partner agencies, including both grocery distribution programs and community meals programs.

Similar to the relationship of the various food programs to the Food Bank, the relationship of the Food Bank to Feeding America is also contractual, with Feeding America mandating sound business practices, food safety and fiscal responsibility. NH has also been represented on the Board of Directors of Feeding America. Good Shepherd Food Bank and the Vermont Foodbank have each been awarded the highest ranking by Charity Navigator, the charity watch dog.

NHFB, the Vermont Foodbank and Good Shepherd Food bank are all emergency responder agencies under the Federal Emergency Management Agency (FEMA).

The NH Food Bank has a number of interesting programs, in addition to its grocery distribution function. When I visited, there was a tantalizingly rich aroma drifting through the air near the food pickup area: it was from the Culinary Job Training Program which is housed in a professional kitchen in a loft area of the warehouse. Under the supervision and tutelage of a professionally-trained chef, a group of under-employed or unemployed adults learn the skills necessary for employment in the food service industry. The program has a high percentage of graduates who go on to full-time jobs because not only do they learn food handling, safety and cooking, they also acquire the cooperative skills of working as a team in a busy kitchen, leadership skills and many others that suit them to employment. One graduate of the program has actually become a professional chef! The program participants are also helped with developing resumes and training for interviews. The food they prepare each day is used in group meals – for example, in the summer months, in the Summer Lunch program. The scent that had my mouth watering was from beef stroganoff. On the menus posted on their bulletin board, I saw popular Mexican and Thai dishes, as well as the usual lasagna and stews. The Vermont Foodbank has a very similar program called the Community Kitchen Academy.

The NH Food Bank grows fresh veggies and herbs in its Production Garden. These are used in the Culinary Training Program, in Cooking Matters (about which I'll talk soon), and if there is enough, distributed to the various food pantries and community meal programs. There is a real appreciation of the importance of the flow from gardens or farms to tables.

Cooking Matters is a program that helps hungry people learn how to eat in a healthful way with limited resources. Unfortunately, many adults in this country no longer know how to cook "from scratch", nor do they know how to shop in a way that stretches their dollars while at the same time giving them more nutritional "bang for their bucks." This program connects hungry people of all ages with resources such as cooking classes, shopping classes, menu planning, recipes and storage and meal extension information, all of which is presented as hands-on experiences. Good Shepherd Food Bank, in Maine, runs Cooking Matters Maine which is a very similar program.

Fresh Rescue is an exciting partnership with supermarkets in each of the states. Representatives (volunteers) from the various food programs collect fresh meats and poultry that would otherwise be discarded. Each supermarket that participates has its own system for ensuring that these important proteins are properly packaged for pickup by the food programs. For instance, Hannaford freezes all of the meats and poultry a day or two before their selling end date, so that the food program volunteers can pick up freshly frozen packages. These are then scanned into the Hannaford inventory database so that Hannaford has a record of the value donated, the weight of excess food and so that no ultimate recipient can bring the meat back to a Hannaford store, planning to cash it in.

The Good Shepherd Food Bank has a program called Mainers Feeding Mainers, in which food producers partner with food banks, pantries and/or communal meals to provide hungry neighbors with fresh and healthy locally-grown food. An example you'll meet in the next chapter is the Friends of Aroostook.

Good Shepherd Food Bank was also selected as a participant food bank in the Rural Child Hunger Capacity Building Institute, a collaboration between Feeding America and C&S Wholesale Grocers. The Institute was initiated in 2015 and its purpose is to formulate programs and approaches to better deliver food to hungry children in rural areas. Twenty member food banks were selected to participate in the study.

Mobile Food Pantries are exactly what they sound like: sort of a Good Humor truck, but one that carries nutritious foods to our neighbors who live too remotely from other food sources. Another analogy that comes to mind is the library-on-wheels that connects many tiny communities with the state library system. The Mobile Food Pantries each provide up to two hundred hungry families with fresh produce and meats/poultry, dairy and canned and boxed foodstuff. As you can imagine, this is a lifeline for many rural poor, who have no transportation and who perhaps live in food deserts. Mobile Food Pantries are active in all three states and help to ensure that some of the most remote residents of the state have access to food. The Mobile Pantries bring food to a central distribution point in a rural area – maybe a low-income housing complex or a church or community center – where people can "shop" from pallets of food. For many, this may be their only way to obtain nutritious food and it is a significant barrier against starvation for many rural poor.

The Lunchbox is a local food truck and learning kitchen that delivers prepared meals and educational workshops to rural, food insecure communities in the

Northeast Kingdom of Vermont. It is a program of Green Mountain Farm-to-School, an independent non-profit organization. While not an agency of the Vermont Foodbank, it deserves mention here.

Maine has the highest rate of hunger among seniors. This is a growing problem everywhere and current data indicates that nearly half of all seniors will have at least one year of food insecurity between ages sixty and ninety. Because of these concerns, Good Shepherd Food Bank also runs Senior Mobile Food Pantries that deliver healthy food to senior housing complexes, senior centers and other places where seniors gather for companionship, entertainment and food. It is hard enough to face the uncertainty of tomorrow and its ills without doing so on an empty belly. For seniors, who have worked all of their lives and contributed to society, it is also a trigger for depression. Malnutrition robs people of their disease-fighting abilities and this is most true in children and seniors, who are relatively helpless victims of hunger.

The Cupboard Collective is a unique cooperative food transportation program that serves those Maine food programs (pantries and meals programs) limited by transportation barriers. These are often in the more rural areas of a very rural state. As in most states, grocery stores are mostly clustered in more populated areas. In 2014, the number of communities served by the Community Collective grew from eight to nineteen. It is a collaborative effort between town government, independent food pantries and the food bank to overcome geographic barriers to food access.

The Vermont Foodbank has three distribution centers, in Barre, Rutland and

Brattleboro. The headquarters is in Barre. The Vermont Foodbank has a unique resource in the Kingsbury Farm in Warren, VT. The Kingsbury Farm is the result of a partnership between the Vermont Foodbank and the Vermont Land Trust. In early 2008, the Vermont Foodbank was chosen as new owner of the Kingsbury Farm by representatives of the town of Warren, the Mad River Valley Localvore Project, the Mad River Valley Planning District, Friends of the Mad River and Vermont Land Trust. The farm is leased to partners Aaron Locker and Suzanne Slomin. In payment for the lease, the farmers provide fresh produce to the Vermont Foodbank to be distributed to pantries and community meals in the Mad River Valley of Vermont.

The SNAP Outreach program helps people who either don't know they are eligible for food stamps or who don't know how to navigate the rather daunting application process. To be eligible, a family needs to have an income at or under one hundred thirty percent of poverty. (See Appendix A) Applying for food stamps is not a user-friendly operation. There is a lot of paperwork and as an average, only about forty percent of northern New Englanders who are in   need have a high school diploma, so education can be a limiting factor in accessing the few government programs available to feed the poor. A great barrier to applying, especially among the elderly, is the perception (confirmed by those I've interviewed) that an applicant is not treated respectfully when applying for government assistance. In Vermont, the SNAP program is known as Vermont 3 Squares.

In July 2015, the New Hampshire Food Bank announced its plan to add a food-processing business to its array of programs to supply both food and jobs/jobs training to the hungry. The concept was developed with a grant from the Entrepreneurs Foundation of New Hampshire and will operate at two levels: one will be the packaging of meals and other food stuffs for distribution through the network of food pantries and communal meals served by the New Hampshire Food Bank. The other will be a line of processed foods to be sold in the retail market under the label "Food Factory." The profit from these sales will be turned back into supporting the mission of the food bank. The processing plant will employ three workers and train them to be competitive in the larger labor market. Only one other food bank in the US operates its own processing facility – Second Harvest, in Tennessee.

All three of these food banks are members of the Feeding America network of food banks – two hundred food banks across the US. Feeding America provides an infrastructure for receiving donated food from grocers, growers, distributors, wholesalers and retailers and portioning this bounty among the discrete food banks. It also provides an organizational framework large enough to perform the research functions that support and inform the various state food banks. In return, the state food banks pay annual dues. Access to donated food is allocated by a system based on the state population and its unemployment rate. It does not take into account the percentage of elderly, disabled or children in a state; this method of computing obviously favors the more populous states – the more urban states.

All of these organizations are voluntary charitable organizations. There are great similarities in how they work – food distribution warehouses and their other programs – but they are each dependent on their own funding and donations. Because of this, the cost of food from the food bank to the food pantry or community meal varies from one food bank to another. Some, like New Hampshire, can sell to the partner food programs for a set per-poundage price, but others, like Vermont, act more like a grocery discounter. Their service to our hungry is invaluable.

Working at the Vermont Foodbank

Farms

Many of us are unaware of the charitable work of our farming and gardening neighbors. Farmers hate to see produce wasted – in fact, most farmers hate food waste of any type. Many New England farms very quietly distribute their extra food to those in need. Most are involved in regular commercial farming, but there are also some farms that exist only to feed those who do not otherwise have access to fresh local produce. Many home gardens "grow a row" to support their local food pantries, as well. The Friends of Aroostook is an example of this charitable farming, although there are many others.

Aroostook County, Maine is nicknamed the "Crown of Maine" because of its position along the northern border of Maine, nestled against the Canadian provinces of Quebec and New Brunswick. Aroostook also means "Beautiful River" and the name gives you a hint of the beauty of this forested land of rivers and small lakes. It is also a hard land on which to live: remote from cities, frozen and snowed in for long winters and lacking many industries to support its people. In fact, the woods and the hardscrabble land are the source of much of its thin economy. It is a large county with an area larger than the states of Rhode Island and Connecticut combined. And poor. Median household income (in 2013 dollars) is thirty-seven thousand, eight hundred fifty-five dollars. More than sixteen percent of Aroostook's people live below the poverty line.

Washington County lies to the east of Aroostook, and is promoted as the "Sunrise

County" because its easternmost point is where the sun first warms the United States each morning. Like its neighbor, Aroostook, it borders New Brunswick, Canada on the north and its eastern border is the Atlantic Ocean; most of the population of Washington County lives along the coast, leaving a vast under-populated area toward the west. In fact, this county is the largest east of the Mississippi River. Its median household income is thirty-seven thousand, two hundred thirty-six dollars (2013).

Blueberries are the life blood of Washington County – work in the fields of blueberry bushes is seasonal employment, to say the least, and the price we pay in the supermarket for Maine blueberries, especially the wild ones, is very inflated above the price paid to the farmer. Workers in the field earn even less. More than nineteen percent of the residents of Washington County live in poverty.

According to a fifty-year-old friend who grew up in Aroostook County, when he was a boy, communities took care of their own by surreptitious "liberation" of potatoes from various local farms. These potatoes were then delivered to families in need and firewood was similarly shared out. He said that his uncle and his uncle's friends were expert deer "jackers" who hunted and butchered a number of deer each year in order to deliver meat to the needy families in their communities. The game wardens were complicit in that they ignored this behavior because they knew where the meat was going. In many of the little villages and hamlets, the churches put together Thanksgiving and Christmas food baskets and delivered them to those families identified as needy by a knowledgeable local source – often the school nurse. I grew up in such a community in northern New York State and went myself with the Catholic Youth Organization, to deliver holiday food baskets. It was enlightening, embarrassing and humbling to deliver a basket to the home of a school friend. She was pumping water from a well, using a hand pump, when we drove into her driveway. She and I were thirteen years old.

In both counties, population is gradually declining, with a decrease of more than three percent in each year since 2010. The percentage of seniors on fixed incomes is, however, increasing.

Seven years ago, in 2008, a non-profit farm organization, called Friends of Aroostook was started through the Empowering Life Center in Houlton, ME. Dale Flewelling, the volunteer Executive Director of Friends of Aroostook, sold his transmission business to his son and devoted his time and resources to growing a farm based on volunteer labor to "feed the hungry in Maine by planting, harvesting and donating fresh fruits and vegetables." In the first year, a harvest of three thousand six hundred ears of corn was donated. Since then, under Dale's leadership, the farm has raised and donated more than two hundred thousand pounds of produce. All labor is voluntary and on a pleasant summer weekend, the fields of the farm are festive with the brightly colored clothes and bobbing heads of the volunteers from as far south as Bangor as they harvest and weed. As well as food, more than one hundred cords of wood has been cut and split to supply heat to seniors of the region.

The food goes to food pantries, community meals and especially to seniors, at senior meals or hand-delivered to their homes in both Aroostook and western

Washington counties. Specifically, it goes to sixteen food pantries in Aroostook County and one in Washington County. Dale and his volunteers recognize the particular hardships faced by the elderly in remote places like northern Maine. The seniors are living on fixed incomes, many with only social security. . and in an area with an average household income around thirty-eight thousand dollars, it tends to be a small social security check. Many have no transportation and public transportation is simply a dream in these remote areas.

In addition to distributing fresh produce as it is harvested, Fred and his crew (four part-time staff during the season, plus volunteers) utilize the commercial kitchen owned by the Houlton Band of Maliseets to process some of the produce for longer storage and winter use. Winter squash was the first crop prepared this way.

The Greater Eagle Lakes project of the farm is a good example of an organization doing its best to bring food and firewood to a "food desert." Greater Eagle Lake is one hundred ten miles from the Friends of Aroostook Farm in Houlton, Maine.

Much of Aroostook County and neighboring Washington County meet the definition of a food desert: a high level of poverty and a ten mile distance from a full service grocery store in a rural area and one mile in an urban area. In many areas of these most northern counties, there are not even convenience stores or fast food places (this is also true in far northern Vermont and New Hampshire). Obviously, if a person has little money and no transportation to a distant market, to maintain a healthy diet is a fantasy. [You can use the Food Desert Locator, a USDA website, to determine whether your home is in a food desert.]

Imagine yourself, a white-haired woman in your seventies, a widow whose children have left the region to find jobs further south, with your annual Social Security income of less than fifteen thousand dollars per year, living in a mobile home that becomes increasingly difficult to heat. This past winter of 2015 was especially difficult because it was so harsh and propane was so expensive. There is no bus to take you to town to buy groceries and no grocery store in which to buy them. You've literally become a hot water (tea is too costly) and toast lady, huddled under blankets in the winter and trying to scratch a garden in the brief summer. Your neighbors are good, but an egg can only be split so many ways.

Veggies for All is a "food bank farm" in Unity, Maine. They style themselves this way because they grow produce to distribute to food pantries and other organizations providing food for the hungry. Sarah Trunzo, director of the program, has said ""There's something about this model that's a little bit too charitable. I mean, we grow veggies just to give them away. But in many ways I feel like it's an emergency when families that live in my community don't have enough food."

Many farms in Maine, New Hampshire and Vermont allow volunteers from food programs to glean their fields after the farm has taken its harvest. Gleaning, defined as collecting excess produce from farmers' fields, is an ancient method of charitable giving that persists today. Most of the time, the farmers themselves don't have time to harvest specifically for donation, because this is the time when they are also trying to feed their own families, directly and by earnings from sale of farm produce, and the growing season involves more than full-time effort .

High Mowing Seeds, in Wolcott, Vermont is unique: here produce is grown for organic seed production. In their Trials Farm, where seed development and perfection is the goal, thousands of pounds of produce are grown. This produce is donated to the Vermont Foodbank.

The Harlow Family Farm, located in Westminster, VT, has been owned by the Harlow family since 1917 and under the ownership of Paul Harlow was certified organic in 1985. It is a diversified farm, meaning that it grows all kinds of fruits and vegetables, poultry (eggs, too!) and animals for meat. Its berry patches look out over the Connecticut River and further up route 5, the cabbage fields are presided over by a huge solar array. From the porch of the farm stand and coffee shop, I've watched a golden eagle soar over the trees and swoop down to scoop up something – a mouse? a vole? - from the recently harvested corn field. Besides being a successful farm that supports many members of the Harlow family, the farm is supportive of its community, employing many local workers, selling the produce of other local growers in the farm stand run by brother Dan, and being tremendously generous to several nearby food pantries. Excess produce is directly donated by the farm to the food pantries and volunteers from the pantries are allowed to glean the fields after the official harvesting. This generates thousands of pounds of fresh produce for needy families in the towns of Rockingham, Westminster and Putney, VT.

Harlow's Farm also has a sugarhouse and a commercial kitchen. In the autumn, when the cooler winds presage the winter to come and the maples are tinged with berry shades, volunteers from Our Place in Bellows Falls, VT are allowed to come to process and preserve produce in the commercial kitchen. This helps ensure a supply of locally-grown produce, processed at the peak of freshness. It also helps the Harlows to have less food waste. Food waste is a grievous thing to anyone who puts in all of the effort to grow food. Farming is a vocation and not just a job . . . certainly there are easier and more reliable ways to earn a living.

There are many farmers in Vermont who are actively involved in supporting the needs of the food insecure people of their own areas, including some more organized efforts, such as RAFFL, Rutland Area Farm and Food Link, whose mission is to build a farm and food system that involves and benefits everyone in the Rutland area of Vermont. Also, as previously mentioned, the State of Vermont in 2012, enacted a law called the Universal Recycling Law (act 148) that mandates any business producing one hundred four tons or more of food waste to recycle it in a tiered fashion, with the best going to food programs for human consumption, the next best to farmers for animal consumption and the inedible waste being composted. Laws like this are necessary in a nation that wastes 34 million tons of food annually.

In Southwestern New Hampshire, the Community Kitchen of Keene enjoys the benefits of having a formal gleaning program This is under the leadership of Sarah Harpster, an Antioch New England graduate whose work is supported by a grant that funded the initiation of this gleaning program. That was two years ago and over these two years, more than sixty-five thousand pounds of produce has been gathered from eighteen local farms, six charitable farms (operating solely for the purpose of supplying food programs), the Keene Farmers' Market and home gardens. All the hard work is paid off by the delight on the faces of the clients filling their bags at the pantry. National surveys have indicated that the hungry would rather make these healthy food choices but are constrained by the cost of fresh food. After all, if a McDonald's meal can cost you one dollar and a pound of broccoli costs two dollars and eighty-nine cents, the person with five dollars in his pocket will buy the McDonald's meal five times and will involuntarily ingest a lot of salt and fat. For a hungry person, filling the belly trumps a careful diet. It is encouraging to note that in each of the northern New England states, attempts are being made to organize information about gleaning opportunities in order to bring together gleaners (volunteer or paid) and farms and gardens with excess to glean.

One of the nearby small farms, New Dawn Farm, has opted to "adopt" the equally small food pantry in Chesterfield, NH – Joan's Food Pantry. Joan's has a Saturday morning distribution, so on Friday evening, Clai Lasher-Sommers and her crew harvest boxes of whatever produce is ready to pick, e.g. zucchini, cucumbers, radishes, lettuce, and delivers it to the pantry early Saturday morning, before the clients arrive to fill their boxes. Many other small farms have similarly targeted their surplus to a local food program.

Some farms who have CSAs (community-supported agriculture in which a participant pre-buys a "share" of the farm's produce) allocate a share or two of produce to be earned by labor on the farm. This allows a family or two of able-bodied people to earn their food directly. Such arrangements could also help older landowners continue to farm/garden after they are not physically able themselves.

All of the food banks, in concert with regional "foodies," have a Farm to Table program. In most instances, this is a fund-raising dinner, featuring local food, donated by local growers, cooked by volunteer chefs and eaten by local people who pay a restaurant price (twenty-five to fifty dollars/per person) for their meal. Usually, there is also entertainment featuring local talent. The proceeds are donated to the food bank and used to purchase food for the needy.

Coos County, NH

I wanted to visit Coos County, the northernmost county in NH, before there was any chance of bad weather, so Chris and I headed north on a sunny early September day. As we drove, the air grew crisper and the trees were already stained golden and red. It was a glorious day. Nearing our destination in Berlin, we could see that we were in a basin between the southern and northern ranges of high peaks, both areas blanketed with the mixed greens of the White Mountain National Forest. Birds were calling; the temperature was just right for a light sweater; it was perfect weather and scenery for a vacation or a day's outing.

We had a late morning appointment with Vickie Plourde, the administrator at the Harvest Christian Church. Vicki is exemplary of the many people we met – mostly women – who are the go-to, take charge people of their organizations. They make it all happen.

Berlin is a small city of less than ten thousand people, nestled along the Androscoggin River. The river and the surrounding forest have been the traditional source of income for Berlin and much of Coos County through forestry, sawmills and paper mills. Over the past twenty-five years, the mills have gradually failed, taking most of the economic wellbeing of the county with them. Today, only one mill, the Gorham mill, is open at all and it is a part-time operation. Today's per capita income in Berlin is around twenty-four thousand dollars and the available employment is low-paying. Most of the county is a food desert, i.e. people have to travel more than ten miles to a full-service grocery store. Berlin residents have access to a super-Walmart and another local supermarket. Many of the more rural communities and isolated dwellings have nothing – not even a convenience store. Tourism brings in some dollars, but they provide a very slim trickle-down and virtually dry up in the winter months.

The Feeding Hope Food Pantry started out as a program of the Tri-County Community Action Program four years ago (2010). It was hosted by them and managed by Kathy, the Community Integrator with Northern Human Services. Kathy supervised and managed the food pantry with her otherwise-abled clients packing the food boxes, providing cheery smiles to food recipients and filling the role taken by volunteers in other programs.

Three years ago, Tri-County CAP (Community Action Program – CAPs originated as programs under the 1964 Economic Opportunity Act) wanted to shed this particular program and the Harvest Christian Fellowship agreed to take on the mission of feeding the hungry. The pastor and board of Harvest Christian Fellowship felt that this was a natural extension of their Christian message. Kathy and her clients still manage the actual packing and distribution of food boxes and Kathy continues to be salaried by Tri-County CAP. Feeding Hope serves the residents of Berlin, Gorham, Shelburne, Dummer and Milan.

The church manages all of the logistics: food ordering, compliances, the physical plant, and fund-raising (food drives, donor drives, grant-writing, etc.). Basically, Vickie does it.

Vickie is a good example of how people make it in Coos County. After having high-power jobs in the technology industries in California, Vickie and her husband returned to the North Country to enjoy the good air, rural life and family. Like many who have made the choice, they knew it would take a different approach to employment to make a living. Being church administrator, including the administration of the food pantry and the soup kitchen, would be called a full-time job by many, but it is a part-time job and Vickie has a similar part-time job with the local library.

In August 2014, the food pantry served two hundred eighty-six families: five hundred seventy-four individuals. Sixty-eight were seniors over age sixty and one hundred seventy were children under eighteen. The previous month, two hundred twenty families (four hundred forty-three individuals) were served. Vickie notes increasing need, especially among the seniors and children. This mirrors what I've heard elsewhere.

The New Hampshire Food Bank has certain minimum food safety standards that must be met by any food program partnering with them, but Feeding Hope has gone beyond this. They have made the commitment and put in the effort to have their soup kitchen meet restaurant standards. Among other things, this means that they are subject to state inspection for compliance with health standards. They also take advantage of food safety classes taught by University of New Hampshire and hosted at the Harvest Christian Fellowship Church.

The community meal (nicer term than soup kitchen, surely) is every Wednesday and serves sixty-five to ninety-five people per week. These communal meals are not subject to means testing. (Two other venues in Berlin serve a meal each week and the Catholic Church serves an additional meal on one Saturday each month.) The fluctuation in attendance is determined by such things as when Food Stamps and other food benefits are distributed each month. Vickie always makes sure that there is a child-friendly, but nutritious entrée available, even if it is just peanut butter or cheese sandwiches. She also makes sure to have enough leftovers to feed the youth group that meets on Thursday evening because she knows that some of the children attend only to be fed. Vickie says that this is a new phenomenon over the past year or so and that there is an increasing number of children, in junior high or high school, who seek food aid on their own. Vickie knows the sad home circumstances of some of them, but not all. She is also disturbed by the increasing number of elders who need the assistance of the food pantry and the community meals.

Vickie has good reason for concern. Currently, seventeen percent of the hungry served in food pantries nationwide are seniors, and twenty-seven percent of those who eat at community meals are in this age bracket. Experts who examine trends to plan for the future predict that by 2025, fully one half of the hungry in this country will be our elders. In other words, our parents, aunts, uncles, older siblings who have contributed to society all of their lives and have tried their individual best to plan for aging in their communities, will no longer be able to provide for themselves the essentials of life. And we hear all the time about what a wonderful country we are – so wealthy, the dominant economy in the world, a world power. And we see ourselves as a major donor to good causes in the developing countries, but our national domestic policies are neglectful and mean toward those who have worked so hard, each in his own way, to build our country.

Currently, the breakdown of recipients of food services in northern New England looks like this:

	New Hampshire	Vermont	Maine
Disabled	55%	57%	38%
Retired	40%	30%	59%
Caretaker/other	6%	13%	3%

Sourced from Hunger in America, 2014 Report

Not all of the seniors planned to retire, but life happened: they were laid off from a job, had an illness that took them from the job market, had a crisis in the family or any of a number of individual disasters. Since 2008, the job market has been very tight and for an older adult virtually impossible. In fact, many were laid off and replaced by younger part-time workers and have either not been hired or have been offered such minimal employment that they are unable to support themselves and their families. Ironically, the income from this marginal employment may make them ineligible for any assistance such as food stamps or fuel assistance

Like all food programs partnering with New Hampshire Food Bank and receiving commodity food from the USDA (distributed through Tri-County CAP), Feeding Hope Food Pantry must determine the eligibility of all recipients. The recipients are screened for income verification (income tax returns, pay stubs, evidence of public assistance, etc.) at their first visit and yearly thereafter. All programs (except communal meals) have to demonstrate at least eighty percent compliance with USDA guidelines in order to be eligible to receive USDA food. As a church, Harvest Christian Fellowship (as well as any other church-based program) has the discretion to give twenty percent of its food aid on a charitable basis to anyone whose individual circumstances don't meet the criteria for the USDA, but are judged by Vickie and the other volunteers to have significant need. The program, like all others that I visited, gives a one-time food box to any first-time applicant. Applicants who don't meet the income requirements are offered budget counseling by parish volunteers who have an expertise in financial management.

Many of the volunteers in this program are themselves recipients of various types of aid and are required to do community service in return for their benefits. Others are minor offenders in diversion programs who are similarly required to perform community service. There is a girls' correctional home nearby for whose residents this is an earned privilege; they enjoy this service and work hard to earn the privilege through their good behavior. The kids who come after school do such things as set tables and serve lighter bowls and platters of food.

Feeding Hope doesn't yet have a Summer Lunch Program but they plan to implement a food distribution center this summer. This would provide children a protein, milk and fruit to take home to provide the nutrition to which the children have no access during the summer vacation. It replaces the school meals that aren't available during the summer. There are Federal funds to help with these programs and grant-writing is another hat that Vickie wears.

Eighty percent of the food distributed is purchased, primarily from the New Hampshire Food Bank. The Food Bank sells groceries to its partner agencies for eighteen cents per pound and delivers the food on the first Tuesday each month to a central location in Berlin, for delivery/pick-up by the various food programs in town. Orders for the food from the food bank are placed online, giving Berlin the same access to inventory as those programs that are physically located near the Food Bank, in Manchester. The remaining twenty percent of food is donated by the various food drives (Boy Scouts, US Postal Workers, etc), excess stock or dinged or post-date cans from the local Walmart, produce from local farmers or purchased using locally donated monies. This is used to buy case lots of groceries at the local Sav-a-Lot. Groceries for the food pantry are kept separate from those for the community meals because the eligibility requirements for community meals are far less stringent than those for grocery programs – all who come can be fed at a community meal. Vickie says that her greatest challenge is that there is never enough food. It is hardest at the end of the month, when individual recipients are most needy and the food is running out for everyone.

The Federal Emergency Management Agency has a budget for emergency food aid and twice yearly disburses funds to food agencies. Each agency submits a request for these funds and has to document what it has spent on food distribution. The United Way evaluates the requests, receives funds from FEMA and divides the funds proportionately among the agencies on the basis of the various requests.

The Harvest Christian Fellowship has a mission statement and feeding the hungry is a mission of the Church. It is through the Church that the food program has its tax-exempt charitable status. Although it is a young program, Feeding Hope is currently writing a plan of operation and a transition plan to ensure its longevity.

Dining Room at Harvest Christian Fellowship Church – all communal meals are served and eaten here.

Ellen

Ellen is a good example of a senior whose situation changed dramatically and drastically after retirement. Ellen and her husband were, as they say, "well set up" and had over a million dollars in their retirement funds. Mark had been an officer in a medium-sized company and had good benefits and stock holdings and Ellen had started a small interior design business after their children had finished school and were independent.

The first three years of retirement were a lot of fun; Ellen and Mark traveled around the US, visiting relatives and old friends and enjoyed being "snow birds" at a condo in South Carolina. They enjoyed a life of good food, cocktail hours, golf, swimming and skiing. And then Mark had his first stroke. He was seventy years old.

They were sitting with friends at a small dinner party, when suddenly Mark became very flushed and his speech became garbled. Initially, Ellen thought he was choking on something, but soon realized that something more serious was happening. The ambulance arrived very quickly and Mark was given the best of treatment, including anti-clot treatment at the local medical center.

Mark did quite well with his recovery and worked hard at physical therapy and speech therapy. He spent six weeks in a rehabilitation facility and then came home to their condo, where various adaptations had been made to help him navigate safely. The bill, when it came, was big, but not alarming. Medicare and their insurance had covered most of it.

Two months later, Mark had another stroke. This one left him more disabled, needing a walker to get around and help with everyday activities like eating and dressing. Ellen was still healthy and vigorous and was able to take care of Mark's needs well, but she did hire an aide to come into their home one day each week to give her respite. Those days were like mini-vacations, Ellen said - times when she could meet a friend for lunch, go to have her hair cut, or simply sit at a coffee shop with a book for an hour. Again, the bills were staggering, but didn't wipe out their available funds.

Almost exactly one year after his first stroke, Mark had another. This one was very crippling and left him unable to walk, communicate clearly or even assist with eating, dressing, using the toilet or any of the things we each do daily. In fact, he was now incontinent. Ellen brought him home and struggled valiantly, with the assistance of the aide, Nancy, who had now become a friend. Nancy came three days each week and Ellen and Mark's daughter drove down from Pennsylvania as often as possible to help her mother. It was very difficult and Ellen began losing weight. She was also sleep-deprived, because she was afraid that Mark would need her in the night. The bills from this hospitalization drained a further chunk from their savings and Ellen began to economize on the little luxuries she had previously allowed herself in order to keep her spirits up.

Soon, Ellen herself became ill – pneumonia. She was hospitalized and the only option for Mark was emergency nursing home placement. Ellen was in the hospital for one week. When she went home to the condo, her daughter Marta came from Pennsylvania to care for her and to assess her parents' situation. It soon became clear that Ellen would no longer be able to take care of Mark and that he was too compromised to be adequately cared for in their home. Marta began the   process of negotiating the red tape of Medicare and personal financial obligations attendant on people entering nursing homes. Ellen was too frail now to take on any of this. She gave Marta power of attorney.

Mark was able to stay in the nursing home in which he was initially placed when Ellen became ill. It was not a luxury facility, with fancy furniture, but it was adequate, with a good staff/client ratio, nutritious food (Mark's had to be pureed and he was spoon-fed) and good access to timely medical care. There was at least one registered nurse on Mark's unit every shift. Marta knew that many nursing homes fell short on some of these criteria. And it was close to the condo, so her mother could visit Mark daily.

Four years later, Ellen fell and broke her ankle. It was a silly thing and she felt very angry with herself. She'd been doing fine on her own and life was as good as it could be, under the circumstances, but she turned her foot on the step down to the parking lot at the condo and fell. She heard the ankle snap. A couple of hours later, the orthopedic surgeon told her that it was a bad break ("are there any good ones?") and that she needed surgery and the placement of some screws. A brief phone call and Marta was on her way.

Thanks to Marta, Ellen only spent two days in the hospital and did her rehab as an outpatient. Marta stayed for a month and arranged for Nancy to come in and help Ellen with meals and getting in and out of the shower safely. Nancy also did the laundry and grocery shopping. It worked. Three times weekly, Nancy drove Ellen over to visit Mark at the nursing home. By the end of the year, Ellen was much stronger and Nancy dropped back on her visits. She and Ellen continued grocery shopping together and combined it with lunch out and a visit with Mark.

Mark was becoming less and less responsive. The doctor said that it was due to the hardening of the arteries that caused his strokes and that Ellen should expect the decline to continue. The doctor was very kind but unequivocal in the prognosis.

Finances were tight now. The nursing home was eating up all of their savings and the other medical bills took their chunk, too. Ellen was in good health but she was lonely now. Nancy was one of the few friends who kept in touch and saw Ellen regularly. Ellen simply couldn't keep up with the lifestyle of her other friends and anyway, she felt uncomfortable in gatherings of couples.

Finally, five years into his nursing home stay [the average stay is only two point six years and statistics tell us that seventy percent of those who reach age sixty-five will need some long-term care. This includes in-home care which is cheaper.], Mark had a massive stroke and died. Ellen was now seventy-six and had been living with Mark's illness for seven years.

One month after the funeral, Marta sat down with her mother and they reviewed Ellen's finances. Most of the one million plus retirement fund was gone. Mark's salary when he was working hadn't been high enough to give Ellen more than twelve hundred dollars monthly in Social Security (the average monthly payout) and the various stocks had been sold already to fund Mark's care. Ellen was in the position of too many surviving spouses - on the verge of poverty.

After pursuing a number of ideas, Ellen moved in with Marta and her family and moved with them to Vermont, which is where I met her. Ellen is eighty-nine now and continues to be in good health. She is happy with her daughter and son-in-law and feels that she contributes to the household by doing some cooking and laundry for the family. She also contributes part of her Social Security check to the family purse each month. The retirement fund of which she and Mark were so proud is a memory now.

Lakes Region Food Pantry

The Lakes Region Food Pantry has been in operation since Dec 2012 and is housed in a pleasant white clapboarded house on Whittier Highway in Moultonborough, NH. It is one of several food pantries supporting towns in the Lakes Region of New Hampshire. The building is owned by the food pantry, which is incorporated as a 501(c)(3) charity.

Lakes Region Food Pantry is unique in several ways. First of all, most of the food programs that I interviewed told me that their greatest challenge was money,.i.e. raising enough money to buy the food needed for their clients and to support the overhead of being there for these clients. Amy Norton, founder and Director of the program, told me that her greatest challenge is time – time to man the program, to fundraise, and to sponsor other programs that also help the clients to help themselves

Active fundraising goes on most of the time. There is an annual auction to which residents of the region contribute goods or services. This is both a community function, at which neighbors meet neighbors and buy each other's good and services and an opportunity for residents to support their own. Also, many of the communities of the Lakes Region are affluent. This is a recreational area with many absentee homeowners and Ms. Norton sends a hand-addressed appeal to all of the homeowners on the Moultonborough tax rolls several times yearly. Most respond, many generously – for many it is a chance to give back to a community that holds pleasant holiday memories for them.

Another unusual feature of the Lakes Region Food Pantry is the thrift shop operated in the front rooms of its building. The proceeds from the thrift shop help pay the mortgage and utilities, as well as providing a source of clean and affordable clothing for the clients or anyone else who wishes to buy. I "shopped" while I was there and found that the clothes were all in good repair and desirable.

Lakes Region Food Pantry does not give out monthly bags or boxes of food. It employs a voucher system, whereby a client is given a voucher for dairy, fresh or frozen vegetables and fruits and fresh meat and/or fish. A client may receive one voucher per month. Excluded are potatoes, frozen meats and fish, deli meats and hot dogs. Two local supermarkets will redeem the vouchers and then send a monthly bill to the food pantry, allowing no actual cash to be exchanged. This system is intended to help clients make their own healthy choices and to help clients learn to budget their food monies.

Also to this end, the program runs cooking classes, called Cooking Matters, in which the clients (or anyone from the community) learn to prepare fresh foods and to extend food beyond a single meal. A good example is buying and roasting a whole chicken (especially when it is on special for one dollar ninety-nine per lb). The next step would be using the leftover chicken for sandwich meat, chicken salad or a casserole. After that, the clients would be taken through the steps to simmer the bones in water, making broth and ultimately, chicken soup. Although this was common in our parents' and grandparents' day, too many today have never learned to cook and extend the usefulness of the food available. Through no fault of their own, many young and middle-aged consumers only know how to heat up prepared foods. The participants in these classes receive a bonus gift voucher to the local Hannaford's supermarket if they attend five of six class sessions.

Feeding Families One Bag at a Time
Lakes Region Food Pantry
P.O. Box 1132 • Moultonboro, NH 03254 • 603.986.0357

___ E.M.Heath   ___Meredith Hannaford

— Dairy, Fresh Veggie & Fresh Meat Voucher —
Value of coupon not to exceed $10.00 DAIRY
Used to purchase only: Milk, Eggs, Cheese, Yogurt
Value of coupon not to exceed $15.00 VEGETABLE
Used to purchase only: Fresh & Frozen Fruits & Vegetables (no potatoes)
Value of coupon not to exceed $15.00 MEAT
Used to purchase only: Fresh Meats & Fish, no frozen, no deli, no hot dogs

Client Name: _____

Non-Transferable   Expiration Date: _____

Client Signature: _____

The Lakes Region Food Pantry serves two hundred forty to two hundred fifty families per month and although the program doesn't do the conventional food boxes, it keeps a supply of non-perishables (donated or purchased) for clients to pick up. All clients are screened and proof of income is required from all heads of household and if applicable, a current letter of eligibility for food stamps. This is reviewed with each family every January.

In 2012, the pantry opened with fifteen volunteers; there are now twenty-five. The criteria for service are passion for the purpose of the pantry and that the volunteer not be currently served by the pantry. Like most of the other pantries that I visited, the philosophy of the Lakes Region Food Pantry is that the more people are involved with the program, the more effective the impact on the region. The volunteers range in age from twelve to around seventy. There is one salaried employee, the director.

There is a strong and active board of directors, which meets monthly ten months of the year, with a less formal exchange of emails in the months of July and August. The board ranges in age from forty-five to seventy and the terms of office (two years each) are staggered so that there is always a mix of established and new members serving. Currently, the board has eleven members. Business is conducted in accordance with bylaws and a mission statement written at the inception of the food pantry. The board is currently in the process of writing a business plan. The board has an annual auction committee and a nominating committee and is also writing a transition plan for leadership roles, in case of need. Although the board members are not actively recruited for salient skills, each does bring particular skills to his/her board work. For example, Cathy Baxter, the president of the board, has worked as executive secretary in several nonprofit organizations and is also experienced as a volunteer at a food program in another state. Board participation is one hundred percent voluntary, with members' compensation being their satisfaction in helping others.

The volunteer pool includes summer residents as well as the year-round residents of the region. High school students also volunteer and earn community service points through their school program. The volunteers are trained by shadowing a veteran volunteer and learning by doing.

Eighty-five to ninety percent of the food distributed here is bought from area grocery stores, some at discount, some not, and about five percent from the New Hampshire Food Bank . There is also a program whereby donors adopt a shelf – i.e. commit to filling a shelf at the food pantry with the particular designated non-perishable. For example, perhaps a local auto dealership might choose to stock a shelf with paper supplies for a calendar year. Such targeted donations provide stability for at least some supplies. Much more food is donated in December than in the rest of the year. This seems more related to the holiday mood prevailing in December than it does to actual need: hungry people need food every month of the year.

Challenges identified by Amy Norton, Cathy Baxter and Janine Broadhurst , a volunteer, are having enough volunteers, outreach in the communities to people in need, teaching people how to make healthier food choices on a very limited budget, coordinating with other agencies in order to avoid duplication of services and to learn from each other, smoothly integrating summer volunteers, and maintaining community awareness of the perennial nature of the need to assist the hungry.

Judy

Judy is a thin fidgety woman who looks worn at forty-five. She has worked hard all of her adult life, mostly in service jobs. She's been an LNA, a waitress and a dispatcher for a taxi company, a truck company and the regional mutual aid. Some of these jobs have given her benefits, most have not and the jobs have averaged thirty hours per week.

Judy first needed food aid when she was twenty-five and has needed it periodically over the past twenty years. She has supported her household of children and a disabled mother for these years and has simply not earned enough to reliably put food on the table. Finally, she lost the last job as a dispatcher and hasn't had any luck finding another. "It's hard when you're middle-aged and they can hire a kid."

"I try not to take any more at a time than we need, but one pantry is just not enough." Judy visits several food pantries within a reasonable driving distance. "Sometimes you feel like you're greedy because you need more."

"I am very grateful for the food pantries. If they did not exist, things would be so much worse. When you have food it makes everything else easier. It is great when towns other than the one you live in help. I am very grateful for this food pantry: here they give you a coupon to Hannaford's for thirty dollars so you can buy food that you can use to supplement what you are missing at home. Plus it is more than I ever received at any food pantry. I am very grateful."

Lakes Region Vineyard Church

It was a chilly day in late autumn, when we lined up with an assortment of people of all ages to await the eight-thirty AM opening of the Lakes Region Vineyard Church Food Pantry in Laconia, NH. The other people seemed to be acquainted and were quietly talking and joking. The tone was similar to that at a concert, church service or other pleasantly anticipated event. We understood when the door opened.

The first thing that greeted the eye, up a short flight of steps – almost like it was raised on a dais – was a table laden with glowing, gloriously colored produce. Even the packaging didn't detract from the beauty of the display. This was this week's 'free table' – overstocked or close to sell-by date produce donated by the local supermarkets.

After checking in at a table adjacent to the door, clients could go up to the table and put their choices of fruits and vegetables in their boxes. Thirty to forty families come each week to take advantage of this bounty and to enjoy the free hot breakfast that is provided on Thursday pantry mornings.

One four-year-old boy was so entranced by the fresh mixed berries available that morning that he barely touched his pancakes. Because the church doesn't yet have its kitchen fully functional (a current project) the hot breakfasts and the hot meal on Monday evenings are initially prepared at the homes of two volunteers and then reheated at the church.

The Lakes Region Vineyard Church began in 1990 as a "house church" in the basement of Pastor Dick and Martha AuCoin's basement in Laconia. The couple agreed that they had a Calling to feed the poor and accordingly, started with a cupboard stocked with some canned goods. Over the years, their church has grown, sequencing through a rented facility in downtown Laconia to the present building in a mixed residential and commercial neighborhood. The church bought this building in 2003. Martha AuCoin said "I don't believe we'd have a church if we didn't feed the poor."

Initially, the church served around ten families; now it serves more than three hundred families. All of these are screened for eligibility before being given any of the food bound by USDA restrictions (USDA commodity food and NH Food Bank purchases) but the "free food" donated by local supermarkets is available to all who come seeking. As mentioned previously, thirty to forty families come just for the free produce and bread. The catchment area for the food pantry is Belknap County (population around sixty thousand). Included in the mix of people from Laconia and the surrounding towns is an international polyglot of refugees. In recent years, the food pantry has served families from Sarajevo, Sudan, Cambodia, Thailand, and Eastern Europe. As a church, the food program receives no assistance from the county and it does not fundraise. All donations are therefore spontaneous and triggered either by being a parishioner of the church or by word of mouth news of the good done. Food is also donated from the Boy Scouts and the Postal Workers annual food drives and from the local Hannaford and Walmart. The median household income for the region is around thirty-eight thousand.

Pastor Dick is clearly the spirit of the church and is innovative and inspiring to his volunteers and board members. He is an interesting man with a Master's degree in Biblical Archeology – as he put it "an expensive hobby!" Under his guidance, the building that houses the church is being renovated to maximize the efficiency of the space, while preserving light and esthetics. Of course, money is tight and when the food program needed a walk-in cooler and lacked sufficient funds, Pastor Dick designed and built one, based on air conditioners, that maintains the required temperature quite adequately and without being an energy drain. He credits the help he received from devoted volunteers. He says that one of the greatest challenges of providing food each week is the sheer physical labor involved. Food is delivered from the Food Bank on pallets and he and another volunteer unload and shelve the food. If a windfall of produce is offered, he and whoever else is available have to collect it, keep it cool and then in the preceding late hours or early morning of the pantry day, display the bounty for the eight-thirty AM distribution.

Seventy-five percent of the food given out is purchased from the SuperWalmart or the NH Food Bank and twenty-five percent is donated, mostly by Hannaford's and Walmart. The supermarkets donate when foods are close to their sell-by dates or if they've been overstocked.

If Pastor Dick is the spirit, Pastor Martha (yes, they are both ordained, as is their daughter) is the heart of the food pantry. She is like the open-hearted mother of a family with the clients who come to the food pantry and is there for any who just need a moment to share and perhaps seek solace. She is sensitive to the little touches that indicate respect, like the homey decor in the women's restroom and the casual hand on a shoulder. She greets everyone and keeps sensitive antennae up for any ripples of dissension. This food program has a different feel from any other that we visited – a feeling of community - and I suspect that much of this comes from Martha Aucoin's style of personal interaction.

There are no paid staff members and most of the volunteers themselves qualify for food aid. Currently, the food program has twenty-five volunteers and many are cross-trained to do multiple jobs. There are also several volunteer lay pastors and the Church itself has a board of Elders that meets twice yearly. Pastor Dick said that transition is provided for by this structure and the cross-training. The board of Elders ranges in age from thirty-two to sixty-eight and is comprised of people with various skills. Their terms are staggered and run two years. Most serve two terms and the gender mix is two-thirds male.

Pastor Dick referred me to:

[31] "When the Son of Man comes in his glory, and all the angels with him, he will sit on his glorious throne. [32] All the nations will be gathered before him, and he will separate the people one from another as a shepherd separates the sheep from the goats. [33] He will put the sheep on his right and the goats on his left.

[34] "Then the King will say to those on his right, 'Come, you who are blessed by my Father; take your inheritance, the kingdom prepared for you since the creation of the world. [35] For I was hungry and you gave me something to eat, I was thirsty and you gave me something to drink, I was a stranger and you invited me in, [36] I needed

clothes and you clothed me, I was sick and you looked after me, I was in prison and you came to visit me.'

[37] "Then the righteous will answer him, 'Lord, when did we see you hungry and feed you, or thirsty and give you something to drink? [38] When did we see you a stranger and invite you in, or needing clothes and clothe you? [39] When did we see you sick or in prison and go to visit you?'

[40] "The King will reply, 'Truly I tell you, whatever you did for one of the least of these brothers and sisters of mine, you did for me.'

[41] "Then he will say to those on his left, 'Depart from me, you who are cursed, into the eternal fire prepared for the devil and his angels. [42] For I was hungry and you gave me nothing to eat, I was thirsty and you gave me nothing to drink, [43] I was a stranger and you did not invite me in, I needed clothes and you did not clothe me, I was sick and in prison and you did not look after me.'

[44] "They also will answer, 'Lord, when did we see you hungry or thirsty or a stranger or needing clothes or sick or in prison, and did not help you?'

[45] "He will reply, 'Truly I tell you, whatever you did not do for one of the least of these, you did not do for me.'

[46] "Then they will go away to eternal punishment, but the righteous to eternal life."

The AuCoins live what they believe.

Pastor Dick also mentioned his involvement in the goals of the Better Together

Initiative, which grew out of the Saquaro Seminar which in turn, was a product of a Harvard University Kennedy School of Government project that focused on civic awareness and community involvement. The premise of this initiative is that social capital arises out of social networks (who knows who) and leads to a ripple effect of social capital (the value of association) being "spent" on community welfare. An example given is the old-fashioned barn raising in which neighbors came together to help each other with projects that would be daunting for one individual or family. Another example is the infant project of time exchanges in which members post services that they are willing and able to perform in return for which they are credited hours toward a service that they need from another member. The basis for all of this is the awareness of being a member of a community and looking to that community for reciprocity of services, social interaction and safety (e.g. the daily phone call exchanged by a circuit of aging friends.) Feeding our neighbors fits well with the philosophy of this initiative, especially if we include the recipients of this charity as helping participants or in other words, as members of this network.

Another project that Pastor Dick is working on is collaborating with other institutions in Laconia to provide showers for the homeless. It should be obvious to all of us that keeping clean is difficult to impossible when one is without shelter, running water and living in a harsh climate. We the public often shun the homeless because they smell dirty, but in most of our communities they have no options for bathing. Pastor Dick hopes to remedy this piece of the problem for the homeless in Laconia.

Pastor Dick showing the meat supply to be distributed to hungry clients.

<u>Mary</u>

Mary is a cheerful and motherly sixty-six year-old woman who volunteers at the Lakes Region Vineyard Church Food Pantry. She has been a volunteer for the past three years each Monday and Thursday.

Mary cooks and serves the Thursday breakfasts at the food pantry. This is an eight to ten hour commitment each week, because on Tuesday, she shops for any supplies needed for the meal; on Wednesday she cooks the meal at her home (another four hours) in preparation for transporting trays of cooked food to the church on Thursday morning. She feeds thirty-five to forty people each week and sometimes buys the food herself because she's "fussy about the ingredients" she uses. This costs her ten to fifteen dollars each week. When we visited, the meal was French toast, juice, coffee/tea, and fresh fruit. The toast smelled wonderfully cinnamon-y and the coffee was very good. Mary is not herself a food recipient, although she will take the occasional loaf of bread or fresh vegetables from the "free" table – food available to all, regardless of income status.

Mary cooks all this food in her small home kitchen and looks forward to the day when the church will have a commercial kitchen (in the plans for the next year). She loves being able to cook for more than just her husband and herself.

Mary's daughter is also a volunteer for the program and cooks the Monday lunch.

For Mary, the perks of volunteering for the food pantry are intangible. "I love the people and I've made a lot of friends – when you help people, you get just as much out of it as you're giving." She has also been a Hospice volunteer for five years. She says, "This is a blessed little church – it's the warmest and friendliest."

The greatest challenge for Mary is stretching the available food. She'd love to be able to do more, if only the monetary and food donations were there. A plea on Facebook brought in more meat and delighted her. Virtually all of the food programs have the same difficulty.

Josiah

Josiah is a handsome young man of twenty-two. He is a member of the Vineyard Church and was invited by Pastor Martha to be involved with the food program more than three years ago. It was clear on observation that all of the clients and other volunteers were very fond of Josiah and he has been given/taken on responsibility for many physical details of the food distribution.

Josiah is a massage therapist and also works as a handyman and acts as the church's janitor. He does not participate as a food recipient, but will take produce or meat from the donated offerings ("free table") once in a while.

For Josiah, the rewards of involvement are great: "it's like seeing God impact people and seeing changes in people over time. For example, people smile who have never smiled. Seeing the restoration of people who have had a hard time. Like seeing myself grow." He values having compassion for those people with a hard exterior, people who have been hurt and are now hurting others.

He says that when he was nineteen he had a very critical mindset; now, he no longer assumes the worst about people and is finding love for them. He says that despite the perception that these people (recipients) are moochers, there are so many people in real need and that it is awesome to be able to give real help. For him, sharing the lives of these other people, even if just for a few hours each week, is a blessing and he thinks it would be an excellent thing to involve more young people.

Pat

Pat is an interesting man. A sixty-nine year-old retired engineer from NH Ball Bearing, he now owns his own tree business and for the past two and a half years he has volunteered five hours each week at the Vineyard Church food pantry. He also teaches Bible studies at the jail.

Pat sees his mission at the food pantry as one of helping the clients and as personal development. He prays for and with the clients, helps with physical tasks such as setting up the produce displays and helps to keep order. For example, he says that sometimes there is not enough food to supply what each person desires and sometimes people take more than their share and he takes on the role of gently speaking to them.

Pat finds Pastor Dick a very good role model and has learned a lot about the level of poverty in this area. The people are not always easy to work with, but he's learning to accept people as they are and has come to love many of the people. He finds that the people recognize this change in him and accept him, too.

One of the most rewarding aspects of volunteering, Pat says, is seeing lives turn around. He's seen people recover from physical illnesses and disabilities and also seen people manage to get a good job and rise from their poverty and be able to give back. He's inspired and fed by this.

The Salvation Army – Portsmouth, NH

My impression of the Salvation Army was bell-ringing enthusiasts asking for donations to be placed in their distinctive kettles each winter holiday season, plus the experience of shopping at several Salvation Army thrift stores. However, at several food programs that we visited, I noted that no mention was made of the homeless among the clients. When I remarked upon this, I was told that "Oh, they mostly go to the Salvation Army."Clearly, I needed to know more about the Salvation Army.

The Portsmouth Salvation Army agreed to help me out by answering my questionnaires and any follow-up questions that may be generated. It was their preference that I not visit them, although they did not refuse to accept a site visit.

In northern New England, the Salvation Army has twenty-two community centers and around two hundred service centers in the smaller towns and villages. The vision of the Salvation Army is "Motivated by the love of God, as a leader in Christian faith-based human services, The Salvation Army is committed to serving the whole person, body, mind and spirit, with integrity and respect, using creative solutions to positively transform lives." I learned that they offer community meals (one client joked that "yeah, we pay by saying a prayer before we eat."), thrift stores, drug and alcohol rehabilitation (in larger centers), faith-based counseling and in many areas, a bed for the night.

The Portsmouth Citadel's food program has been in operation for fifty years. The

Portsmouth Salvation Army has a strong advisory board that oversees the food program and a paid caseworker. It operates within the broader vision and guidance of the The Salvation Army structure and serves the towns of Portsmouth, Newington, and Greenland, New Hampshire and Kittery and Eliot, Maine.

Breakfast is served at the soup kitchen every week day, Monday through Friday and dinner is served on Saturday and Sunday. Any who come are fed. For many homeless people, this is their only source of food because they have no access to cooking facilities. Thirty to forty families pick up food boxes that are sorted and packed by volunteers. Confidentiality is expected and staff members do sign confidentiality agreements. Volunteers are directed to respect the privacy of the clients, but don't interact with clients very much –"they just sort food and put it away."

Justin Finn has been a board member of this program for the past three years and got involved through the local Rotary Club. He is currently the Chairman of the Board and brings to it his community connections, an ability to fundraise and a strong work ethic. He is motivated to help others and to give back in appreciation of the gifts he's received in life. For him, the greatest challenges are "competing with the other non-profits and going after the same people who contribute their money and time. We have a lot of good organizations and worthy causes in our community so [it's important] to be different and bring a uniqueness that makes people think of The Salvation Army." The board meets monthly and the age range of the members is thirty-five to seventy-two. Its composition is mostly male, with one woman board member. All members bring unique skills and talents and work

in a variety of industries.

Deb

Deb is a warm and giving woman who volunteers eight to ten hours per month at her church food pantry in Concord, NH. She is middle-aged and volunteers with her husband and her teenage daughter. Deb's daughter painted and generally 'spruced-up' the waiting area at the food pantry as a part of her senior project at Bow High School. She has also hosted fundraisers to purchase hygiene products for the food shelf. (Hygiene products, such as sanitary napkins, diapers, soaps, shampoos and laundry detergent are in short supply at all of the food programs that we visited.) This caring young woman is now away at college.

In Deb's own words:

"There have been times in my life when I have needed a hand up, emotionally, spiritually, financially. I have been so blessed to have received so much that it gives me joy to provide to others and perhaps brighten the day of our clients."

Her greatest challenge is not having enough to offer to the clients, although they are always grateful for what they receive.

The program's weakest point, in Deb's view, is that "there is no money in the "budget" to purchase hygiene products to offer to clients. We rarely have any unless they are donated by a church or other group."

"I so often see that our clients, who have so little, will reach out to help others at the food pantry, whether it is helping to carry their bags out, offering something from their own bags, offering to volunteer as a way to give back, blessing us for our generosity, even though I don't feel that we provide nearly enough."

Capital Region Food Program

The Capital Region Food Program is an interesting program. It began in 1974 as the Holiday Food Basket Project initiated by the Kiwanis Club of Concord, NH and the Interfaith Council of Churches in Concord. This initial effort served one hundred families with holiday food boxes.

As good ideas tend to, this one grew and expanded and in 1984, became the Capital Region Food Program, a separate non-profit organization, with Mark E. Manus credited as founder and chairman for life. Manus, a local restaurateur had an innate interest in feeding people and through his years in business, had made many contacts who were tapped to help with this project, notably, Manus' friendship with the De Moulas family who own a regional chain of supermarkets. To this day, the Capital Region Food Program receives both donated and purchased food from the De Moulas' Market Basket grocery chain.. Monies were – and continue to be – donated by many capital area residents and businesses. The listing of the board of the Capital Region Food Program reads like a "Who's Who" of Concord.

Mark Manus died in 1989, leaving the food program with a void that needed to be quickly filled. His daughter, Maria Manus Painchaud, was voted the new director and stayed in office for the following seven years. During her tenure and with her expertise, the food program was organized along business lines, with a five-year succession plan, layered financial management, board development and strategic planning. It did however remain an all volunteer organization, a fact to which

Painchaud points with pride. Painchaud is an Associate Professor in the School of Business at Southern New Hampshire University and has brought her skills to the organization that was her father's dream.

The Capital Region Food Program is unique among the programs that I visited in that it is a sort of hybrid animal: not really a food pantry and not really a food bank, but with elements of both. It has maintained its original program of holiday food baskets and every December, food is shipped from the Concord Market Basket to the Armory in Concord where volunteers divide and box the foodstuffs for distribution to individual families. Currently, around two thousand families are served and about sixty percent of the program's budget is used for this. A special relationship has existed with the National Guard Armory since the early days of the food program and the Guard has allowed the food program to use its facilities for food distribution for many years. This holiday box distribution is the only time the Capital Region Food Program volunteers interact directly with client families.

The program itself has no physical home – as mentioned, it uses the Armory for its food collection and distribution point. Much of the administrative detail passes through the law office of Susan Leahy, one of the board members and Comptroller.

One of the great contributions of the Capital Region Food Program is its organizational model which it has shared with a number of younger food programs. This shows the younger programs how to apply for 501(c)(3) status, make a transition plan, set up bank accounts to protect access, keep records, etc. These are the essential, but non-glamorous aspects of setting up a viable food program.

Capital Region Food Program has served as a good older sibling to many other programs and remains willing to share its expertise. For example, Capital Region Food Program was very helpful to The Community Kitchen in Keene, NH.

In 1992, a Year Round Distribution Project was formalized. This provides for a monthly distribution of bulk foodstuffs to eighteen area communities, with a total of thirty pantries and food programs. The food is bought from Allied Independent Grocer of New England at a discount and provided at no cost to the participating programs. The communities served are Allenstown, Boscawen, Bow, Canterbury, Chichester, Concord, Contoocook, Dunbarton, Epsom, Hopkinton, Loudon, Pembroke, Penacook, Pittsfield, Salisbury, Suncook, Warner and Webster. For many of these communities, the Capital Area Food Program is the largest source of donated food; many also buy food from the New Hampshire Food Bank and operate their own food drives and fund-raising campaigns.

Maria Painchaud sees that the greatest strength of the Capital Area Food Program is that it is entirely a volunteer effort, but that this is also its greatest challenge. She says that such programs tend to rely too heavily on the same few people and need to encourage the participation of many volunteers to allay burn-out. The organization has been led by her family since its inception, but leadership may pass out of the family after the tenure of Maria and her husband.

Henniker Food Pantry

Henniker, New Hampshire is a pretty college community that hugs the Contoocook River as it meanders through the heart of town. Along the main street, there are pizza and ice cream shops, little gift shops, convenience stores and a fine restaurant whose deck overlooks the river. The parking for the college fills a crescent along the opposite bank of the river. In winter, the river is ice-choked and narrowed, and in spring and summer, the stream is shallow, but fast, with swirls of confused currents and overhanging foliage from trees along the banks. In any season, it is beautiful and the town seems too serene and prosperous for any residents to be hungry.

Historically, Henniker, like many towns, had a fraught relationship with hungry people. It had a poor farm on which the poor and hungry were basically incarcerated and forced to farm and raise their own food. The poor farm burned in the 1920s. Poor people were also given a small sum of money and escorted from town, to take the face of hunger elsewhere. In the 1970s, a small group of women from the Congregational Church laid the groundwork for a community food pantry. By 1980, the townspeople of Henniker realized that the town needed a more realistic and compassionate approach to their hungry and so began the official Henniker Food Pantry, a 501(c)(3) charity. The pantry is only open to residents of Henniker and this, as well as USDA eligibility, is checked yearly. Today, Henniker is an affluent community, with a median household income of around sixty-five thousand.

*The Henniker Grange Building -
home of the food pantry and the office of the social worker.*

Like the town, the home of the food pantry is gracious; it is the Grange building
and looks like a church, white-clapboarded and with a bell tower and steeple. It is
toward the western margin of town and has plenty of parking. People can come
once weekly and over the years, the number of people served has grown. Currently,
around fifty people come each week to "shop." This means that around one
hundred thirty people (household members) are served weekly. Volunteers also
deliver bags of groceries to shut-ins and those who can't negotiate the stairs at the
food pantry.

Denise Getts, a very pleasant and energetic woman of middle years, is the current coordinator of the program and oversees around thirty-eight volunteers. She is a member of a board of seven. There is no paid staff. Denise is a very efficient and organized person and the food program has benefited from this. All the databases are electronic, making it very easy to check a client's eligibility and when they need to recertify (yearly). All the food pick-ups and volunteer assignments are also easily available from electronic files, as are records of donations and purchases.

You also see her hand in the intuitive and user-friendly organization of the very small basement space in which food is stored. There are shelves around three-quarters of the room, and a rack in the center space, creating an illusion of aisles. The food is organized by type on the shelving and labeled with a sign saying "take one" or "take two" or whatever suits the circumstance and the rack in the center space contains the "free" food – donated food that is not restricted by USDA regulations. Like all of the programs we visited, the Henniker Food Pantry gives food to all comers at their first visit while documentation is pending.

Denise has seen two developments over recent years that have increased the use of the food pantry. One is an influx of homeless people to a Henniker campground, where they are 'rented' space by the owner. Although only fit for summer camping, this group of people live year round in tents or lean-tos, with makeshift cooking facilities, and marginal arrangements for sanitation. They are very grateful for the food offered them by the Food Pantry and for the respectful manner in which they are treated.

The other development is the increase in hunger among the elderly. In Henniker, there is a senior living complex, White Birch, and increasingly, its residents need supplemental food from the pantry. Many of these seniors do have food stamps, but it is hard to have an adequate diet on $160 per month. Fran is both a recipient at the pantry and a volunteer. She is seventy-five years old and was an accountant at her job in Florida. A couple of years ago, she moved to New Hampshire with her kids to help them start a business; it took all of her retirement savings. Like most people who have enjoyed a higher standard of living, Fran found it very hard to admit that she needed financial help at such a basic level but learned that she was automatically eligible when she began living in HUD housing. Her income from her pension and social security is slightly too high for her to qualify for food stamps, but not enough to support a good diet. She now lives in White Birch and comes to the pantry to supplement her pension and to feel that she's part of a giving community. Fran volunteers thirty hours per month at the pantry and at the housing complex and feels good about giving back to others. She writes all of the thank you notes to donors and tries hard to make each unique. She marvels at all of the people who donate and says that she can see no weak points in this program.

In a video made about the Henniker Food Pantry (available on YouTube), Denise comments on the quality of food donations: some people seem to be cleaning out their own shelves and give want they don't want, but others give very generously of prized items. She mentions a woman who brings twelve dozen eggs to the pantry every few weeks and others who bring baked goods and makes the point that not all donations need to be non-perishable. The pantry is very happy to receive baked goods, fresh produce from gardens and eggs. The clients were also delighted to receive eggs – the number prorated by family size. An egg can be cooked over a campfire. . . if you have a pan.

Sharon also lives in White Birch and volunteers there. She is a very pleasant former teaching assistant aged sixty-six and retired on SSI disability. She has needed food aid since she was fifty-nine and has lived in HUD housing for ten years. Sharon found applying for assistance very humiliating and difficult and was dismayed that the trauma of her illness was compounded by the way she was treated when she applied for SSI. Like most applicants, she had to apply more than once. She is grateful to the volunteers at the food pantry who respect her as a person.

Denise noted that when the program was inspected by a representative of the New Hampshire Food Bank just a few weeks prior to my visit, the rep remarked that the Henniker Food Pantry is one of the few rural pantries that give out food on a weekly basis. She (the rep) also remarked on how clean and bright the space is – thanks to good lighting, light-colored paint and frequent cleaning – and the layout of groceries so that people can feel that they are "shopping."

Denise considers that the mission of the Henniker Food Pantry is to ensure that "everyone in our community has access to enough nutritious food to feed themselves and their families. We accomplish this by acquiring and distributing food to those in need. We envision a time when no neighbor goes to bed hungry." Although this is not yet the formal mission statement, Denise is currently working on this and a transition plan to put in place when it is time for her to move to another activity.

Carol Conforti-Adams is the town social worker and every recipient of food from the pantry must see her at least once yearly. People are channeled to her office when they come for food and she is able to help them access aid through other available programs, such as SNAP, WIC, the Free School Lunch and Breakfast programs, etc. In some cases, her role is to make families aware of the programs available to help them (e.g. the child nutrition programs). This was the only program we visited that has a resident social worker. Feeding the hungry utilizes a complex web of interacting private and public resources which are easiest to navigate with the trained services of a social worker. Henniker has recognized this.

Rochelle is seventy-two and gives around nine hours monthly to the food pantry. She is retired from Osram Sylvania, where she worked as a trainer. She is impressed by the kindness of the volunteers who staff the food pantry and by how well-organized it is. She is very happy to be part of the volunteer staff. "It's gratifying; I feel like I've helped out." She also helps to deliver bags of groceries to the homes of shut-ins and seniors and has given rides to clients who have no transportation. She says that it is nice to be able to help others.

St. Thomas More Food Pantry

St. Thomas More Food Pantry is a ministry of St Thomas More Catholic Church in Durham, NH. Durham is also the home of the University of New Hampshire and St Thomas More hosts the Newman Center of the University, so the food pantry benefits from student volunteers.

St Thomas More Food Pantry, like so many others, was started by the efforts of a small group of people, an effort spearheaded by Tom Dolan. It began in 1988 and initially operated from a storage closet in the church hall and served four to six families weekly. Today, Tom Dolan and Cynthia Racic serve as coordinators for the pantry. Each has organizational skills that complement those of the other.

The pantry is still located in the church hall but it occupies much more than a storage closet. Clients enter a large bright space and are greeted by two volunteers who are seated at a table that indicates the line between the waiting area and the distribution area. St Thomas More is by far the most organized pantry we visited and new clients are given a package with the guidelines for participation, and the questionnaires that determine eligibility. The emphasis is on honoring the dignity of the patrons as the necessary information is gathered to determine USDA eligibility. [USDA commodity food can only be given to those people who meet the income guidelines, but as a church, the pantry serves anyone in need in a caring and non-judgmental manner.] The guidelines address such issues as snow days, smoking and parking policies and the care of children accompanying patrons. It obviously works because when we were there, the small children were very well-behaved and occupied with small toys and books. Electronic databases, easily accessible to the volunteers, also track all volunteer assignments.

A unique feature of this pantry is the random assignment of a number to each patron (the preferred term at St Thomas More). The patron is to wait in the waiting area until his number is called and then he's welcome to enter the distribution area and take his choice from the "free" table. When we were there, the "free" table was piled with bakery goods donated by a local market - breads, cakes, pastries, lovely goodies dripping with chocolate. I watched a woman and her young daughter choose a loaf of fresh bread and a pink-frosted cake. The little girl was dancing and singing in delight at this treat. I followed this family as they "shopped." The next step was a room with a Dutch door where they told the volunteer which canned goods and pasta/cereal products that they wanted. Next they were given a share of household products (detergents, paper products, etc.) according to what was available. These are in short supply and not always available. The last stop was to receive their allocation of eggs, dairy and meat or poultry. Patrons may visit the pantry every other week and it's emphasized to them that this food should supplement their shopping. The standard box content is the equivalent of three days of three nutritious meals and snacks. However, for some of the people with whom I talked, this was their only source of food. The pantry served more than twelve hundred families last year and averages twenty-four families each week. It serves the towns of Durham, Dover, Newmarket, Lee, Madbury, Barrington and Somersworth, New Hampshire.

The relationship between the food pantry and the university is beneficial to all – students have the chance to give back to the community and to learn about their greater society, with all its warts and wounds. Over the past year, the food pantry has enjoyed a unique bond with the nutrition program at the university as student nutrition interns have been placed with the food pantry.

POSSIBLE SAINT THOMAS MORE FOOD PANTRY INTERNSHIP ACTIVITIES

1. Develop a questionnaire to determine food and nutrition related client concerns, issues, questions and suggestions to improve Food Pantry service and/or offerings.

2. Develop a course(s) of action based on the feedback from #1 above

3. Explore ways and means of making the application for and processing of food pantry clients easier and more efficient, i.e. food pantry software ???

4. Work at least three sessions to include meat distribution, pantry distribution and shopping cart deliveries. Provide an evaluation and recommendations based on your experience.

5. Research and develop a list of organizations that could/would use food that is excess to the STM Food Pantry requirements.

(courtesy Tom Dolan)

Since many patrons have the nutritional diseases of poverty – obesity and diabetes – the interns both have good learning exposure and good opportunities to use their skills to help the patrons, both individually through nutrition counseling and collectively, by writing monthly newsletters full of food tips and recipes. These newsletters are printed in color and in an easy-to-read font, so they are attractive and easily available in the waiting area of the pantry.

St Thomas More participates in the Fresh Rescue Program of Hannaford's and Walmart. This is a formal program whereby the supermarkets donate food that is near or at sell-by date. All meat and poultry is frozen (usually the night before its sell-by date) and must be picked up and stored in the pantry's freezers in an efficient manner. Hannaford's requires a contract with the food pantry ensuring that all food is appropriately handled and that inventories are kept and reported to New Hampshire Food Bank on a monthly basis. St Thomas More receives two hundred to three hundred fifty pounds of meat from Hannaford's each month. They also receive breads and pastries. They buy enough eggs, cheese and yoghurt each week to supply thirty client families. The rest of the food is mostly purchased from the New Hampshire Food Bank or received as donations from various food drives. The work of the volunteers is not limited to pantry days or to signing in patrons and distributing food. There is a lot of unseen work in picking up food donations from markets, sorting the food and date-checking it and storing it in the refrigerators, freezers and on the shelves. It is a lot of work and much of it is heavy work. There is also the unglamorous work of filing reports with the New Hampshire Food Bank (ditto for the Vermont and Maine food programs) every month and with the USDA quarterly.

St Thomas More has a wish box for patrons to submit suggestions and wishes for particular items to be available. In March of 2014, the requests were for:

1. Some Baby Food; Formula, Cereal, etc. Note: only 1 request
2. More Ground Turkey and Chicken
3. Vegan products
4. Fresh/Frozen vegetables: Spinach, Cauliflower, Broccoli, Lettuce, Tomatoes, Asparagus
5. Orange Juice
6. Skim Milk
7. More Hamburger
8. Bread Crumbs

And patrons requested the following types of recipes:

1. Recipes to enhance a bland cancer diet for both nutrition and taste
2. Meal and dessert (sweet) recipes for Diabetics and those with Hypoglycemia.
3. Cheerios recipes
4. Healthy school snacks
5. Homemade granola

6. Recipes for crockpot meals

7. Veggie recipes

8. Homemade soups

9. Spaghetti sauce

10. Pork chops and Applesauce

11. Croutons (with day old bread)

12. Bread Pudding: Sweet with apples, fruit, nuts; Savory with Peppers, onions or ham and eggs

13. Lamb

One volunteer told the story of a young woman who came in to pick up food and was most annoyed because tofu, bean sprouts and protein shakes were not available. "I just decided to become vegetarian and take better care of myself and you're no help at all!" Usually, the patrons are very grateful for the food available and thank the volunteers. Several said that they are very careful about being greedy because they know that others need the food, too. Others told me that they have themselves donated non-perishable items that were given to them, but that they don't like. . . "it should get used."

We met with Kirstin, a twenty-two year-old senior at University of New Hampshire, who is one of two nutrition interns currently at St. Thomas More. She works four hours per week at the pantry, counseling individuals, making menus and recipes that utilize the available food and to meet special needs, such as diabetes or homelessness, and giving cooking demonstrations. Kirstin has volunteered at another food pantry and works part-time as a cook at a long-term care facility in Manchester, NH. Kirstin said that she likes volunteering at St. Thomas More because "the atmosphere is very relaxed and the people are very appreciative. It is also a way to donate to others." She plans to become a registered dietitian and to work with community outreach and nutrition education in the community.

Zack is another twenty-two year old volunteer. He is a graduate student and teaching assistant in environmental engineering and has volunteered four hours weekly at St Thomas More for the past two years. He finds that the atmosphere of kind volunteers, good organization and grateful clients helps him to "de-stress" from his studies. He suggests that a delivery program for shut-ins would be a good addition to the current efforts of St Thomas More.

An interesting side note is that full time college students are not eligible for food aid under any of the Federal food assistance programs.

Durham has a median household income of around sixty thousand dollars per year. This is close to the state median household income of around sixty-four thousand dollars per year.

Michael

Michael Rozumek asked that he be identified by his full name because he wanted his story told. Michael grew up as the child of a master carpenter and a full-time homemaker. He followed his dad into the union and was himself a master carpenter for thirty-eight years. "But I blew it. I liked bad company, drink and drugs and eventually, it caught up with me. I lost my job because of irresponsibility, lost my marriage and hit the skids."

" I woke up to having diabetes and no job or home. I have two kids at home – aged fifteen and sixteen and two others are grown and on their own. At about the same time that I got sick, my parents also became unable to care for themselves. Both have dementia and my dad has had several strokes. I moved back home with my two kids. I went from earning about fifteen hundred dollars weekly to applying for food stamps. All my own fault. This year, I also got fuel assistance. I've been 'retired' for three years now."

"And things got worse. I've been diagnosed with terminal pancreatic cancer and told I have maybe six months to live. I've applied for Social Security Disability (I'm fifty-four) and now I'm playing that waiting game. It'll probably come through after I die. Pride just goes out the window when you get this low."

Michael went on to say that if it weren't for the food pantry, he and his family couldn't eat. He tries to make sure that they use all of the food that he takes and if there are items that don't get opened (cereals) he passes them on to someone else. He said that he wanted people to know that you need to take care of your life and that he accepts all responsibility for where he's at. "I guess this can be my memorial."

Our Place Drop-In Center

Bellows Falls, Vermont was a mill town, and today the old buildings still overlook the Connecticut River, but have been repurposed. Some house various artistic endeavors in space made available at a subsidized rate by the town government. Our Place Drop-In Center occupies a low brick building on what is known as "the island" – an area of land in the Connecticut River and connected to Bellows Falls proper by two bridges. It is a near neighbor to the Amtrak station and the trains rumble by at regular, but infrequent intervals. The building is not large, but efficient use is made of the available space. When I visited, I entered a cheery yellow room, in which tables and chairs awaited the lunch hour. One man was sitting and reading the local newspapers and a woman was doing some needlework. To my right, at the end of the table area was a sitting room, with comfy chairs and a corner designated for children's play. Lisa Pitcher, the director, told me that the children's corner was started in recent years by the founder (1992) and original director of Our Place, Donna Stevens. Stevens had become aware that some of the children served by the program for their food needs had such marginal housing that they had no place to play. Since play is vital to children's social and intellectual development, Stevens resolved to make a safe place for them.

The kitchen, under the professional management of Chef Matt, is perpendicular to the table area and against the wall separating this room from the rest of the building. Matt and his helpers prepare and serve ten meals weekly – breakfast and lunch each weekday. Originally, Stevens served meals from the tailgate of her vehicle – an unusual "tailgate party." The food pantry is open daily from 9 until 4, but is closed for lunch each day. The day I visited, Matt served up a tasty, healthy and colorful lunch of African peanut soup, a mixed green salad from the community garden across the road, and carrot coins. Dessert was spice cake.

Behind the kitchen wall is the rest of the building: a food storage area that occupies around two-thirds of the north wall, two very small offices, and the food pantry area with its array of shelves, fridges and freezers. Squeezed in between is a small bathroom, where guests may shower, if they need and desire. Lisa said that it is used frequently.

This building is rented and Our Place pays heat and utilities. A relatively recent frustration has been the purchase of the building on the other side of a parking lot to the north. The new owner installed barriers to the parking area that make it impossible for the Food Bank truck to deliver into Our Place's storage area. A foreseeable problem is that the Rockingham Development Office has plans to develop Green Island, the plot of land on which these buildings stand, into a "green" industrial park, providing sustainable employment for the area. Obviously, this will force a move by Our Place. It is easy to understand why Lisa says that the physical facility is the program's greatest challenge.

In 2013-2014, Our Place served around two thousand different people. Currently, they serve over five hundred people (one hundred forty-five to one hundred fifty families) each month and deliver to around forty homebound people (ill, old or disabled). Numbers increase slowly, but steadily each year with five to fifteen percent increase in demand for services over the past three years. (Median household income in Bellows Falls is around thirty thousand dollars per year. Vermont's median household income is fifty-two thousand five hundred plus.) There was a large increase in need between 2009 and 2011, with a forty percent increase in use of services. Currently, the demographic breakdown is twelve percent seniors, thirty-eight percent children, thirty-five to forty percent disabled, and fifteen percent currently working – an additional thirty-four percent have worked recently but are currently unemployed. They are included in the previous numbers. These families come from the Towns of Rockingham, Westminster, Grafton, and all of Walpole, NH, including North Walpole (separated by a foot bridge from Bellows Falls) and Drewsville, NH. The Town of Rockingham budgets five thousand dollars yearly to support the work of Our Place in giving sustenance and succor to its residents. Fifty percent of the funding for Our Place comes from individual donors with the remainder from grants from private foundations and state grants.

Many times, clients need a lot of services and besides a warm welcome and a non-judgmental shoulder on which to cry or lean a little, the volunteers and staff of Our Place also help people to fill out applications for Vermont 3Squares (SNAP or Food Stamps), fuel assistance, subsidized family housing or senior housing, as well as other programs. Although one can apply online for many of these programs, this is not much help to a person who has no computer or Internet access at home. If she has a home. Also, documentation needs to be copied to mail or fax to the appropriate agency and Our Place helps with this, as well. The volunteers who help to make all of this happen range in age from early thirties to seventies and Lisa can count on a steady pool of ten or eleven volunteers at any one time. Lisa also works with an involved board of directors, which is currently eight people.

Lisa Pitcher carrying a food delivery

Careful databases are kept by a part-time accounting employee and the finances are audited yearly. Lisa herself has a business background and an eye for detail.

One thing that impressed me very much in talking with Lisa is the collaborative spirit on the Vermont side of the Connecticut River. In New Hampshire, the food programs that I have visited or discussed with others are all pretty much islands unto themselves. Not all directors are happy with this, but time and distance mitigate against greater cooperative networks. Just across the river, the food

programs along the Connecticut River from Springfield to Brattleboro, including

Bellows Falls, Grafton, Chester/Andover, Westminster, Putney and Dummerston

are exploring the benefits/disadvantages of a loose coalition. They have named this

the Healthy Harvest Network and have received a grant (Lisa was one of the grant

writers) from the Fannie Holt Ames and Edna Louise Holt Fund for the purpose

of studying the ramifications of this idea and the implementation of it. Among

other functions, it would facilitate the sharing of excess donated groceries among

these programs without necessitating the involvement of the Vermont Foodbank.

For example, pretend that the Putney Food Shelf was given six flats of blueberries

by a local farmer; the Putney Food Shelf serves a very small population and those

blueberries would volunteer themselves into jam before they were fully distributed.

However, just down the road in Dummerston, there are many families who would

love to enjoy blueberry pancakes, so the blueberries could be transported by a

volunteer from Putney to Dummerston. Many bugs, such as transport, will be

addressed in the study.

Area farmers have also been tremendously supportive of their hungry neighbors.

For example, the Harlow Farm, in Putney and Westminster, is a certified organic

farm that has been operated by the Harlow family since 1917. It has been certified

organic since 1985 and is locally and regionally recognized for the excellence of its

produce, eggs, chicken and meats. It is less well-known how helpful the Harlow

family is, individually and collectively, to their neighbors. For years, they have

offered the excess from their fields to the local food pantries and they allow volunteers from Our Place to glean their fields of pounds and pounds of produce that might otherwise go to waste. At Harlow's Sugar House, there is a commercial kitchen and Our Place volunteers are allowed to use this at harvest time to process and freeze produce for the winter months when little might be available for the clients of Our Place. This relationship is precisely what some of the directors of other food programs dream about.

Lisa Pitcher is proud of the work done at Our Place, but she saddens as she remarks that their work should be unnecessary – no one should need to worry about her next meal in this wealthy country of ours.

Seacoast Family Food Pantry

The Seacoast Family Food Pantry is the current name of a philanthropic food program that has existed for two hundred years, originating as the Ladies Humane Society in 1816, and chartered by the NH legislature in 1874. The organization has changed its name five times over the years, and became the Seacoast Family Food Pantry in 2007, with a mission of striving "to fulfill the needs of low-income individuals with food, personal care products and education for healthy living." "These services are provided on both an emergency and an on-going basis, respecting the dignity of each individual." Services are provided to Portsmouth, NH residents and the people of the surrounding seacoast area, including Greenland, Hampton, New Castle, Newington, Rye, Seabrook, and Stratham, NH and Kittery, Maine.

Like most of the programs we visited, the Seacoast Family Food Pantry is an incorporated charity and depends on the generosity of donors – individuals, businesses and foundations. Deb Anthony, the Executive Director, has a mandate to grow the organization in a thoughtful and progressive manner with a goal of serving more people and with an eye to the need to find a larger space for the food pantry. Currently, the pantry is housed in a wing of the old City Hall building. This space is convenient to the Department of Human Services, for those food pantry clients who qualify for various government programs, but it is small and will revert to the city in a few years. It does have the advantage of the summer Farmers' Market being held just across the parking lot. However, the need for more space will soon be critical; in 2007, the food pantry served fifty to seventy households per month. Today it is serving more than three hundred fifty households per month. There has been a ninety-two percent increase in seniors needing service in the past two years (since 2013).

Margie Parker is the Operations Manager. She not only supervises the stocking of the shelves and refrigerators, but she also oversees the flow of individual "shoppers" as they fill a bag or carton with nutritious food. She has a "staff" of fifty volunteers, twenty-five of whom are active in any given week. They range in age from six to seventy-five. As in other programs, clients are screened yearly for eligibility and reports are filed with the USDA and the NH Food Bank. Only thirty percent of the food here is bought; seventy percent is donated by arrangement with local supermarkets, by food drives and by donations from individuals and organizations. In fact, as we entered the building, the first thing I saw was a rainbow display of bouquets, donated by the nearby Trader Joe's. I later learned from a client that this is a monthly gift to uplift the spirits of the clients of the food pantry..

Deb Anthony has a dream for the future of the Seacoast Family Food Pantry; she would like to partner with local farms and process their produce to add value and shelf-life to the food. She envisions this as an off-shoot of the pantry, with clients having the opportunity to participate in the food-processing and profit from the end products and from learning the process.

Obviously, a program that has persisted for two hundred years has had a successful mechanism for leadership change and Deb told me that the Director serves for one or two three-year terms and that the organization is currently involved in writing a transition plan for the board of directors. There is a board handbook so that each board member does not have to learn by trial and error. Also, the terms of the board members are staggered so that newer members have the benefit of the experience of the longer-serving.

Jeanne Haskins, Treasurer of the Board, points with pride to the Summer Meals 4 Kids program that provides ten meals per week for those children who depended on free or reduced-price school lunches during the school year. This program not only provides these children with food, it also teaches them to recognize more nutritious choices of food and helps them toward food self-sufficiency by teaching them how to prepare simple, but nutritious meals. There is also a Meals 4 Seniors program designed to serve the rapidly increasing number of seniors who are food insecure. This program provides Senior Only Pantry Hours twice monthly. This enables those seniors who prefer to "shop" in a less crowded setting to do so. Also, to respond to the more urgent needs of seniors who cannot or are unwilling to visit the pantry, bags of healthy prepackaged foods are delivered to locations, such as senior centers, senior housing, churches, etc., from which volunteers can privately deliver them to the seniors in need. It is hoped that these services to seniors will expand to include more service to shut-ins, transportation options and more pantry hours.

<u>Suzy</u>

Suzy is a fifty-seven year old former schoolteacher who studied economics. Ten years ago, she was forced to retire because of illness and now lives on her Social Security disability. She is a vibrant, bubbly woman who has never married and has lived alone in the same apartment for many years. Although unable to work, she tries to "give back" by volunteering at many cultural events in the city of Portsmouth.

Because of her educational background, Suzy is very adept at budgeting her money, but even so, she only has forty dollars left from fixed expenses each month with which to buy food. Her disability income is too high to allow her to receive food stamps or any other federal assistance.

Most of Suzy's income is eaten up by rent (seventy-six percent of her income) and medical expenses and she doesn't dare let go of her old car or her cell phone plan because they are her link with the world and her firewall against emergencies. For Suzy, the clear choice is between rent (a reliable roof over her head) and food.

"I love food," Suzy beamed at me, "and it shows." (She's what used to be called 'pleasantly plump.') "No one looking at me would think that I rely on the food pantry, but I love my own cooking and I know how to make the food last."

As a visual demonstration, she showed me some pictures: one of an almost empty fridge (one bottle of catsup stood on the shelf) and the other of a fridge with greenery frothing out of the shelves. "That's kale that was donated to the food pantry. I use every bit of it. I chop the stems and cook them in soup and I freeze any kale that I can't use immediately. I use all of the food this way."

At Christmas, the pantry receives special donations of meats and it is a huge treat for recipients to be told to "pick a meat" for their holiday celebrations. Suzy said that "I couldn't treat myself that well" after being given a high-quality steak for her Christmas dinner. There are also special holiday flower arrangements donated by Trader Joe's and Suzy said that she takes photos of them each year in order to remind herself that unseen people care about her welfare – both physical and emotional. The flowers are a tremendous boost to her spirits.

When I asked Suzy how it felt to initially apply for food aid, she said that it was very hard. She felt that there is a great stigma attached to not being able to provide adequately for herself. But like others, she had no choice, so she had to swallow her pride.

Suzy is passionate about not wasting food and hates to see any waste. She also expresses gratitude for all who donate to food programs; they save lives and also benefit by the self-esteem generated from giving to others. It is very important to Suzy to be able to "give back" in as many areas and as often as she can.

Chris

Chris is a thirty-seven year old mother of three whose family has needed food aid for the past year. She had been working as a para-professional in a medical office, but the demands of a special needs child meant that she had to progressively cut her hours of work until finally, she was terminated. She had been earning what she considered a good wage and so had her husband Mike, but he was "downsized" at about the same time that she was fired and he's been unable to find new employment since. The family also lost their medical benefits with Chris' job. The kids are now covered by New Hampshire Healthy Kids program and Chris has applied for Medicaid for herself.

For the first year of their unemployment, the family subsisted on Mike's unemployment benefits, pulling their belts tighter and tighter, with both adults skimping and skipping meals to feed the children. Finally, when Chris felt tired and light-headed all of the time, she realized that she had to look for help. She applied for and immediately received food stamps – "it was easy. I guess we needed it so bad that they didn't give us a hard time." This plus the food pantry is how she feeds her family now. She is especially grateful to be able to sometimes get paper products, like toilet paper and disposable diapers from the food pantry, because she can't use food stamps for these. Her oldest child is six and her youngest is two. Because the family has no car, it is difficult for Chris to get to the food pantry or the grocery store and she has to rely on friends. The lack of a vehicle is also an impediment to her husband's job seeking.

Chris is also very grateful to all the people and businesses who donate to the food pantry: "without them, my family might starve."

The Community Kitchen, Inc.

Keene, NH is a lovely small city, nestled in the depression of an ancient lake bed and surrounded by hills. The Ashuelot River runs through and it is overlooked by Mount Monadnock. Its economy has evolved from manufacturing which has left the city with an old money base, to one based on low environmental impact industries, such as insurance, education and the arts and fine crafts. Its population of around twenty-four thousand is expanded each academic year by students at Keene State College, Antioch University, and River Valley Community College.

In 1982, two Keene State College students, Mindy Cambiar and Tony Guglielmi, attended the Chicago Federation for Progress convention in Chicago. While there, they attended a session on how to start a food bank. This was all it took to ignite the fire in Mindy's belly and on her return they talked with local charitable agencies in Keene and with the Capital Region Food Program who shared their wisdom and paperwork necessary for the inception of a food program. Soon, the Community Kitchen was a reality on paper, with 501(c)(3) status and its first board of directors: Dwayne Mitter, Arthur Scott, Mary Jensen, Lee Conroy, and Mindy as the first director of the Kitchen. The first meal was served in July of 1983 at the St James Episcopal Church as a project of the Church's mission committee. Twenty-five people showed up for the first meals, and within a couple of years, the number was more than two hundred. Soon, the Unitarian Church hosted an additional meal per week and then the United Church of Christ served a meal on Sundays, making hot meals available to the hungry on four days per week.

The organization struggled with space, need for more food donations, paperwork and money. In the beginning, they relied on donated food from stores and restaurants, competing with the area pig farmers. C&S Wholesale Grocers was a major donor and the Kitchen received grants from Catholic Charities and the NH Charitable Foundation. Soon they had to comply with means testing for clients in order to be an agency of the NH Food Bank and to receive USDA commodity food, distributed through Southwest Community Services. Mindy was initially the only paid employee and the meals and pantry left her with only scraps of time for her family and friends. After a couple of years, another employee was hired to do the cooking and cleaning. By 2006, when Mindy retired, there were thirteen full and part-time employees.

During the years of growing pains, there were several moves of the pantry to larger spaces, donated by Tim Robertson and Chris Tsoulas and then a move to the old Princess Shoe Factory on Water Street. Meanwhile (in the early '90s), the Church Women United became more and more aware of the wear and tear of serving community meals in the churches. It was their policy to pick a mission each year to support and for which to fundraise, so they decided to purchase a permanent home for the Community Kitchen. This would serve the mission of feeding the hungry, while at the same time, relieving wear and tear on the various churches. As a result, in 1994, the current building on Mechanic Street in Keene was purchased and renovations begun. The Kitchen moved into its permanent home in 1998. It is the hub for the Pantry program, which distributes food boxes weekly on Wednesdays and Thursdays, as well as the Hot Meals, serving six meals each week – an evening meal on weekdays and lunch on Sunday. The most recent addition to these programs is the Gleaning Program which began in 2013. This program partners with a number of other local agencies, businesses and individuals to operate six charitable gardens in the Keene area, with produce targeted for the Kitchen. It also works with eighteen area farms and gardens, allowing Kitchen volunteers to glean produce after the official picking by the farm workers, garnering hundreds of pounds more fresh produce to be distributed to hungry families and to be used in the Hot Meals program. The Pantry program requires verification of income and residency for each recipient, but the Hot Meals are available to anyone.

Today, the Kitchen still has thirteen paid staff, but the volunteer pool has expanded to one thousand, with an active core of about one hundred volunteers. Their age range is five to ninety-four. Phoebe Bray, the current director, says that it is heart-warming to see the five-year-old boy so carefully pick a potato or box of pasta to hand to a client . . . and it makes clients smile. Phoebe says that today about five hundred families are served weekly. They are primarily from Cheshire County, with some from contiguous counties. No residents of other states may be served by the pantry program (i.e. they cannot leave with a box of groceries), but they are welcome to eat at the Hot Meals. The Hot Meals feeds more than seven thousand people each month.

Phoebe talks of the problem of the young and the old – young people who are now on their own and have no idea about how to make a budget and use their monies wisely. And the elderly (some not so old) who are not desirable in the job market, have no pensions and are trying to live on Social Security. Many did manage their money wisely and saved for retirement, but had tremendous losses during the Great Recession. These are losses which they cannot recoup in their remaining lifetimes. Some of the money-savvy volunteers do give their time to help people plan and budget their money so that these working poor will one day be able to pull themselves up into a more comfortable economic situation. This is not the situation for the seniors; they know how to budget and have done it for a working lifetime, but the economic environment has changed and they have seen the comfortable cushion they worked so hard to acquire just plain deflated. Some had pensions which were lost in company restructuring or bankruptcy or IRAs or 401(k) plans that dissolved in the market meltdown. Some have seen a partner's illness further erode funds. It is a hopeless place to find oneself at sixty-plus. One thought that Phoebe expressed was to team seniors and young working poor to allow the young to benefit from the budgeting knowledge of the seniors and the older persons to benefit from the energy and physical strength of the younger people. This would at least help with some of the isolation of being poor.

It is Phoebe's dream for the Community Kitchen to own and operate a farm. She sees this as an opportunity for the clients to be intimately involved in producing food that nourishes them, both in body and spirit, and as a way for the greater community to approach the problem of hunger as a reality in its midst. Money – or lack thereof – stands in the way.

The greatest challenge for the Community Kitchen is fundraising for both money and food, and Phoebe's job is often a drudgery of trying to pull together resources.

There are some consistently generous donors, notably Fenton Family Dealership, Hannaford's and Market Basket, as well as individuals, but there is still a huge need for the community to embrace its role in feeding its less fortunate. Many people have a burst of generosity at the holidays because they are infected with the gifting spirit of the Thanksgiving-Chanukah-Christmastide, but forget that the need does not go away during the rest of the year. In fact, January and February are months when donations seriously drop off (people are paying their credit card bills from the holidays) and there is a much greater need in the summer months when the school children are no longer eating breakfast and lunch at school. Sherry, a senior volunteer at the Kitchen says "Hunger never goes away. Hunger increases and supplies don't. People forget the need during non-holiday times." He and Linda, another volunteer, speak of their gratification at feeling they've helped people and also of the warm relationships that they've formed with some of the recipients. Sherry says, "You look forward to seeing certain people and miss them when they don't come. When they return, you feel a great relief."

The Kitchen has gone through the growing pains of changes in leadership and now has a written plan for this and to meet other exigencies. Ann Heffernon is a board member and she says, "Nothing could have prepared me for the challenges of joining this board. We have grown by leaps and bounds, but I came in at a time when we were on the edge financially, had extreme problems with staff, morale and leadership. We have come so far . . ." Her greatest satisfaction is seeing that the Kitchen is at a point where it is truly supporting those in need, while at the same time, she is saddened by the increasing need.

Federally-funded Programs

Although much of the support of food aid to the food-insecure in America is voluntary – in other words, from private pockets like yours and mine – there are some government programs that provide much needed support for less-privileged individuals and families. The following chart gives an outline of these programs and what each does and who it serves.

Name	Description	Mothers & Children	Seniors	Nutrition Education	Supplying Food banks
Supplemental Nutrition Assistance Program (SNAP)	Provides monetary coupons to low-income families to be used for groceries	Yes	Yes	Yes	
The Emergency Food Assistance Program (TEFAP)	Provides USDA commodity food through food banks to families for short-term emergency food relief	Yes	Yes	Yes	Yes

Name	Description	Mothers & Children	Seniors	Nutrition Education	Supplying Food banks
Commodity Supplemental Food Program (CSFP)	Provides monthly USDA commodity food to low-income seniors	Yes	Yes	Yes	Yes
Child & Adult Care Food Program (CACFP)	Provides meals & snacks for children & adults in designated care centers	Yes	Yes	Yes	
National School Lunch Program (NSLP)	Provides school lunch to income-qualified children	Yes		Yes	
School Breakfast Program (SBP)	Provides school breakfast to income-qualified children	Yes		Yes	

Name	Description	Mothers & Children	Seniors	Nutrition Education	Supplying Food banks
Summer Food Service Program (SFSP)	Provides free meals & snacks to low-income children during summer months	Yes		Yes	
Women, Infants & Children (WIC)	Provides nutrition education and food to low-income women & children at risk	Yes		Yes	

Source: usda.gov

What do we mean by commodity supplemental food? The commodity food program is a function of the USDA and provides a monthly box of nutritious food stuffs to specific classes of at-risk people: those over sixty, children under six and those women who are pregnant, postpartum or lactating and who are not served by the WIC program. The foods included are canned items (fruit, vegetables, meat or fish), bottled juice, ultra-pasteurized milk and instant dry milk, cheese, pasta or rice, dry beans or peanut butter and cereal. Recently, the USDA revised the offerings to make sure they were lower in fats, sugars and salt. Approximately ninety-seven percent of the recipients are elders whose income falls at or below 130% of the

Federal Poverty guidelines. For 2015, one hundred thirty percent of the poverty threshold is one thousand two hundred sixty-five dollars gross income (before-tax income) per month for a single person and two thousand five hundred eighty-four dollars gross income for a household of four. These income guidelines apply for all of these federal programs.

The SNAP coupons are known as Food Stamps. Today these are commonly in the form of a debit card (EBT card) that is less stigmatizing than recognizable coupons fluttering in the hands of a person standing at the grocery store check-out counter. Food Stamps can be used to buy any foods that will be consumed by the household, including protein foods, such as meats, fish, poultry and beans; grain foods such as breads, rolls and cereals; fruits and vegetables and dairy products. Seeds and starter plants can be bought with food stamps because they will produce food for the household. People cannot use food stamps to buy beer, wine, alcohol, tobacco, marijuana where it is legal, pet foods, household paper products (including disposable diapers or sanitary products) or cleaning products, supplements or medications or prepared foods that are eaten in the store. The latter prohibition is sometimes relaxed, allowing the homeless, elderly or disabled to use SNAP benefits to obtain inexpensive meals at restaurants. This relaxation of the rule recognizes that people in these categories often find it difficult to impossible to prepare their own meals at home and might subsist on unheated food directly from cans. Also, many recognize that the socialization inherent in eating in community, whether it is a group meal at a food program or at a cheap restaurant, is important to the mental health and social skills of people who may be marginalized or isolated.

Linnet is a forty-four year old woman whom I met when doing her pre-employment physical exam. I'd never seen anyone quite as excited by a new job as she was. "This is my dream job," she exclaimed. "It will pay more than minimum wage [it pays nine dollars/hour] and after three months, I'll have benefits. It's a temporary position, but I just know they'll keep me on." Linnet is a single mom who was unable to work full-time when her son was young. "It was a catch twenty-two: I needed to earn more to afford day care, but day care was twenty miles in the opposite direction from my work, so it just didn't make sense." Her son is now independent, struggling with low wage work in another state. Linnet's elderly mother lives with her and has little money to contribute to the family budget. Linnet never wanted to apply for assistance and just talking about it made her tear up, but "without food stamps and the food pantries, we wouldn't be able to eat anything. . . I also take my mom to the meals in Brattleboro sometimes, like at the end of the month, when the money's gone." Linnet's previous job as a school bus driver gave her a decent wage per hour, but provided only twenty-five hours of work each week that school was in session, giving her a yearly income of just under thirteen thousand to feed and house her mother and herself. In Vermont, according to the National Low Income Housing Coalition, it takes an hourly wage of twenty dollars and sixty-eight cents for a family to afford a two-bedroom apartment. Clearly, that was and continues to be beyond Linnet's reach. She and her mom live in a studio. He mom has a bed and Linnet sleeps on a futon.

My close friend Lulu is a good example of the growing plight of seniors. Lulu is sixty-eight and has worked hard in her own business all of her life. She felt reasonably secure and was able to provide a solid middleclass upbringing for her son. Suddenly about eight years ago, things began to go awry. Lulu fell and broke her arm and was unable to work for the six weeks that she was in a cast; her business fell off. As the nation's economy slid into the Great Recession, so did Lulu's and she found that all of her retirement savings had disappeared, her house needed costly repairs and she couldn't work long hours anymore because she'd developed severe arthritis in her neck. Her social security check barely covered her monthly bills. Lulu spent her nights huddled in blankets to conserve heat, crying in hopelessness. Son Robert was in no position to help her – he was a fresh college graduate trying to make it in the very thinly-spread job market. One night when she was more depressed than she could ever remember, she realized that she had to 'adjust her attitude' and ask for help. Lulu had always been a giver and to accept help, let alone ask for it, was foreign to her nature and upbringing. "I was lucky," she now says; "I just dropped in at the Social Services office in Keene (NH), and asked this nice woman to help me. I think she was the supervisor, but she seemed to be alone that day. She asked me a lot of questions about my income, what I had in savings (down to nine dollars!) and my expenses. She was very gentle with me and could see that I felt totally humiliated and emotional about this. She said that I still needed to send documents verifying my information, but she could tell me that I'd be eligible for not just Food Stamps, but also for fuel assistance, some sort of medical card that helps with my prescriptions, and with dental care. She gave me a list of the documents that I needed and said that I'd receive my EBT card in about a week after the application was complete. I went home and collected all of the things I needed – Social Security payments, utility bills, fuel oil bills, property taxes, etc. [see Appendix B for list of documents needed to apply for SNAP] and went to the library to copy them all. The next day, I went back to Keene and delivered all of the proof. My EBT card arrived one week later."

Lulu went on to say "having the Food Stamps has made a huge difference for me. I can buy milk and eggs now and good vegetables. I still buy my meat at the local market because they have good meat, but I don't eat a lot of it. My diet is better and that makes me feel better."

The statistics show that most people use the SNAP program for about two years. Lulu has just applied for her third year and this will most likely be the pattern for our elderly. We elderly will not be helped by a better jobs market or an increase in the minimum wage. We will experience the rising cost of food, just as everyone else does, but our income is fixed and many of us will need to rely on SNAP and voluntary food programs indefinitely. It is a very sad reality that none of foresaw as we did our work, gave to our communities and raised our children.

The value of the food stamps disbursed is determined by the cost of a hypothetical basket of food for a family of four, shopped according to the Thrifty Food Plan (see the USDA website), and is pro-rated for those households of more and less than four members. It is also age-adjusted, with the value for a family of four children under age six currently at five hundred sixty-nine dollars and forty cents and for a family of four with children over the age of six entitled to six hundred fifty-four dollars and ninety cents per month. A man of fifty to seventy years of age receives one hundred seventy-one dollars and fifty cents per month in food stamps, whereas a woman of the same age receives one hundred sixty-one dollars and ninety cents. Men get a raise after age seventy, currently one dollar and thirty cents/month, but women over seventy are cut by three dollars and ten cents/month. This is presumably because of differing calorie requirements for men versus women and smaller versus older children.

SNAP does save lives and the statistics do show that it contributed to raising five million Americans out of poverty in 2012. Many of these people were victims of the "Great Recession." Access to Food Stamps has also been shown to improve health in low-income people.

We have in recent years heard a great deal of jaw-flap about economic stimulus packages and other ways to revive an ailing economy. According to a study by Moody's Economy.com, and economist Mark Zandi, the fastest and most efficient way to stimulate the economy is to expand the SNAP/ Food Stamp program. He observes that each dollar in Food Stamps is spent immediately and that this dollar then ripples through the economy, helping to pay the salaries of grocery workers, the truckers who transport the food, farmers who produce the food and through these workers, the dollar further expands the economy through their subsequent purchases of goods and services. Each food stamp dollar generates one dollar and seventy-three cents in economic activity. This is not a hypothesis – it has been demonstrated to be true.

USDA research shows that each five dollars of Food Stamps is nearly doubled in increased economic activity by this ripple effect. In 2009, the USDA looked at how much the addition of eligible, but non-participating households to the Food Stamp rolls would impact the general economy in the individual states. In New Hampshire, the addition of five new households to the Food Stamp rolls would increase economic activity by thirty-six hundred dollars; in Vermont, this was twenty-two hundred dollars. Eighty percent of Food Stamp recipients are either working or not expected to work (children, the disabled, seniors).

A frightening reality is that each person between the ages of sixty and ninety today is projected to endure at least one year of hunger in his/her remaining lifetime. And by 2025, one half of the SNAP eligible people will be seniors. The face of hunger soon will be that of your grandmother or your father. . . or mine! My friend Lulu is a good example – you might say she's ahead of her time. Lulu was never wealthy, but she was secure. She is a pillar of her community and owns her own business. Because of a number of health issues related to her osteoporosis, Lulu is not able to work as many hours as she once did, so she rented out a room in her house and sold her mother's jewelry. Property taxes went up and so did fuel oil prices. . .each year. The "Great Recession" hit and like so many middle-class people, Lulu watched her retirement funds evaporate. Much of her savings had gone to pay medical bills before she was eligible for Medicare. Now, at least, she has Medicare and isn't terrified every time she walks down the stairs for fear of a fall that would totally wipe her out.

It should be noted that striking workers, college students and some legal immigrants are not eligible for SNAP benefits, regardless of their income. Illegal immigrants are not eligible at all.

The Food Stamp program is two point seven percent of the federal budget. The rate of fraud in the SNAP program is one percent. One in five American children is in a family receiving food stamps. Last year (2014), Congress passed the 2014 Farm Bill which contained eight point seven billion dollars in cuts to SNAP benefits. This followed a 2013 cut of five billion dollars. This translated to an average ninety dollar/month decrease in benefit per family. For comparison, we budget one percent for foreign aid, fifty-five percent for defense and six percent for education. The bureaucratic mechanism for running the government itself is budgeted at six percent of the 2015 budget. SNAP represents a commitment to eradicating hunger in America, giving struggling families an opportunity to get on their feet. It makes no economic, moral or just plain common sense to cut a program that directly stimulates the domestic economy while at the same time, benefiting the health and wellbeing of our own families. What are we thinking? Or maybe, not thinking.

TEFAP is utilized whenever there is an occasion of acute and exceptional need (emergency) such as the flood that happened in my home town of Alstead, NH in 2005 or the ice storm of 2008 that immobilized many communities in northern New England, leaving thousands of households without electricity or heat for several weeks. In these situations, the emergency food boxes are distributed by local or regional agencies, such as food banks, Community Action Programs, or the Red Cross, with the aid of local volunteers, police and fire departments. Individual emergencies may also qualify, such as a fire, loss of employment, etc.

The bulk of the commodity food to which low-income seniors are entitled is delivered via local voluntary programs, like food pantries, and prepared meals using commodity food (Meals on Wheels, Friendly Meals, etc.) We've already visited a number of these programs and you should have a feel for the various ways they are run. Although each program has its unique features, they all ensure a basic amount of food (usually three meals/three days/per person for each recipient family) to households in need and are mostly run by volunteer effort and with additional donated food and funds.

CACFP provides reimbursement for food provided at adult day-care centers, at-risk after school programs, child care centers, and group homes. They mandate that the monies provided be used to provide nutritious snacks and meals and CACFP provides educational resources to help programs meet this goal.

The National School Lunch and School Breakfast programs have become increasingly important in the feeding of our children. The income guidelines are set at one hundred thirty percent of poverty for free lunch and between one hundred thirty and one hundred sixty-five percent of poverty for reduced-price lunch.

In 2000, only thirty-eight percent of public school children were eligible for free or reduced-price lunches, but today, the figure is more than fifty-one percent. This is pointed to by media such as the New York Times and politicians such as Senator Bernie Sanders, VT, as indicative of the increasingly downward mobility of our population. The disturbing reality is that an increasing number of our children rely heavily on these programs and many are hungry from the time they leave school on Friday until they hurry to school for breakfast on Monday. When eleven-year-old Ethan was caught rummaging in dumpsters behind the grocery store in his town, he was fortunate that in our small rural communities police recognize a child's need versus delinquency and Ethan's only consequence was a ride home in the squad car after being treated to a sandwich – a gift from the cop. Hunger and malnutrition rob a child of his ability to focus and learn and may also contribute to behavioral problems, ultimately depriving the child of achieving his full potential; this in turn robs us of a fully-contributing member of society. It also leaves children more vulnerable to disease and society to the increased costs of hospitalization for these children. Also, in larger communities, feral children who rob dumpsters are often treated like criminals and not as the desperate young people that they are. Growth and development are as difficult without nutrition as it is to run a car without gas.

The Summer Food Service Program recognizes the need of low-income children for food-security during the school vacation months. Under this program, local organizations provide hot meals and distribute backpacks with healthy snacks to eligible children. The meals and distributions occur at child-friendly venues, such as Boy and Girls Clubs, the YMCA, churches, libraries or similar venues. This ensures the child at least one well-balanced hot meal each week day and some are augmented by back pack programs that provide an assortment of easy to prepare meals and snacks for the child to eat over the weekend. Hunger doesn't take a vacation. It is a shock to realize that eighty-four percent of the children who receive free or reduced school lunch do not have access to summer meals. This program is mostly implemented in our more urban areas, although some rural communities host it at churches or schools. The limiting factors are 1) recognition by a community that it has a childhood hunger problem, 2) a safe and child-friendly venue, 3) a gifted member of the community who will organize both the logistics of such a program and do all the paperwork to apply for the grant monies to fund it. Or preferably, more than one person to ensure smooth running. I recently heard some community organizers talking about another barrier to the summer lunch program: there should be more activities available to occupy the children, such as a summer camp, a reading program, an exercise program, etc. As always, in our rural areas, transportation is a huge issue and children are much less likely to be transported just for a meal – important as this is – than they would be for a program that essentially provides childcare for a number of hours. Too many of these children have working parents who can't take time to bring their children to a meal site in the middle of the day, but would be delighted to have safe childcare for the work day.

Ethan

Ethan is eleven. I met him at a community meal, where he seemed to be on his own. He reminded me of the children that Vickie Plourde in Berlin, NH had mentioned –those who forage on their own because of difficulties in their homes.

Ethan told me that he's okay during the school year, but whenever there is school vacation, he is hungry. With enthusiasm, he described some of the school breakfasts, including his favorite one – pancakes with little sausages. His favorite lunch is pizza and he's happy to have an apple for dessert because he can save it for later. At home in the evening, he sometimes makes a dinner of canned soup, if they have any in the house or crackers or dry cereal. Lots of days there is nothing.

Ethan's mom "sleeps a lot. She's has bad headaches and she takes too much medicine" he told me. His dad is in prison.

 Ethan's town does not participate in the Feeding America Backpack Program that provides children like Ethan with a weekend supply of convenient and nutritious food or the Summer Lunch Program that provides a hot meal for low-income children each week day during the summer vacation. These programs are funded by grants from the USDA Food and Nutrition Service and it is unconscionable that only one in seven children who qualify for free or reduced-cost school lunches attends these programs. Many communities and most individuals with whom I've spoken are unaware that they exist. So children go hungry.

Ethan's father is in prison on drugs charges and it is possible that his mom's "medicine" is also an illicit drug, but this is not Ethan's fault, nor that of any child in these circumstances. Children like Ethan are human bundles of potential and if we as a society don't maximize the chances of that potentiality being realized in a positive way, then fie on us. Ethan has already been caught stealing (food, of course) and is ripe to develop as a petty criminal or, if nourished and nurtured, as a teacher, counselor or other contributing member of society. Every child needs the care and resources of an involved community.

There are more programs available for children than there are for seniors, but many of them rely on someone at community level finding out about them and having the leadership skills to put them into operation. This alone is a huge impediment to access for all eligible children.

The Women, Infants and Children program (WIC) provides supplemental foods (see below), education about nutrition in pregnancy and for babies and children, and healthcare referrals for low-income women who are pregnant, post-partum and/or breastfeeding and to their infants and children under five years old. Low-income in this case means one hundred eighty-five percent of poverty level, for example, a monthly income of eighteen hundred dollars for a pregnant single woman or three thousand fifty-one dollars/month for a family of three. In 2014, WIC affirmed its support for breastfeeding by providing professional and peer counseling and educational materials, increased supplemental food packages for those mothers whose infants are exclusively breast-fed, and lactation paraphernalia, such as breast pumps and nipple shields. Breast-feeding mothers are also allowed to be WIC participants for a longer period of time than non-lactating mothers.

WIC-Eligible Foods:

Breakfast Cereal	Infant Cereal	Infant Food Fruits & Vegetables	Infant Food Meat
Infant Formula	Exempt Infant Formula	Milk	Cheese
Tofu	Soy-Based Beverage	Mature Legumes	Peanut Butter
Fruits & Vegetables	Canned Fish	Whole Wheat Bread & Other Whole Grains	Juice
Eggs	WIC-Eligible Nutritionals, e.g. Liquids for Tube Feeding	Yogurt	

Source: usda.gov

Not all cereals and baby meats are created equal. The cereals cannot exceed a specified sugar and salt content and the meats can't be mixtures of meat and vegetables or nuts or other non-meat foods. There are also standards for the breads, fish and juices. See Appendix C for the food packages for infants, children and women.

A number of studies addressing the impact of the WIC program on infant mortality report a significantly decreased infant mortality in babies on WIC. Infant mortality is one of the key indicators of how well a nation's health care system works, and the US's infant mortality rate is an embarrassment.   What is infant mortality? It is the death of a child under one year old. We are twenty-seventh best compared with other wealthy countries (OECD – Organization for Economic Cooperation and Development).   And Slovenia, Singapore and Sri Lanka have better infant mortality than we do. Emily Oster of the University of Chicago and her colleagues Alice Chen of the University of Southern California and Heidi Williams of MIT have found that the higher U.S. mortality rates are due "entirely, or almost entirely, to high mortality among less advantaged groups." Or in other words, inequality begins before birth. African-American women are afflicted by a rate of twelve point seventy-four infant deaths per thousand – almost twice the national average. This is a true disgrace. Since ensuring adequate maternal nutrition in pregnancy, as well as early prenatal care, has been well-demonstrated to reduce the risk of infant mortality, WIC programs are vital to infants, especially with the help given to encourage women to continue breastfeeding. Breastfeeding has itself been shown to decrease infant mortality and morbidity. It is known that WIC participation reduces low-birth-weight births by twenty-five percent and very low-birth-weight births by forty-four percent. Low birth weight is predictive of poorer outcomes for babies (illness, failure to thrive, infant death.)

Women who participate in WIC have been shown to have fewer premature births. Prematurity is one of the greatest risks to a baby's life and can have long-lasting impact on his/her health. In general, the babies born to WIC mothers and who have themselves received WIC benefits are healthier. When one considers the cost of caring for childhood illness and especially, the costs associated with prematurity, WIC is cost-effective, with estimates that each WIC dollar spent saves one dollar and seventy-seven cents to three dollars and thirteen cents on Medicaid spending for health problems associated with prematurity or early childhood illness.

What is in a WIC package? Each package for children age one through four contains juice, milk or a milk alternative like soy milk, cheese or tofu, cereal, at least half of which must be whole grain, cheese, eggs, a cash voucher for fruits and vegetables, whole grain as breads or grains, canned fish and dry or canned legumes or peanut butter. The amounts vary with age and lactation status. Infants (by definition children under one year of age), except those who are exclusively breast-fed, receive a package containing WIC baby formula and at age six months, all infants receive infant cereal, fruits and vegetables as baby food, and baby food meats. The amount of baby formula included is adjusted according to the baby's age.

In 2014, New Hampshire had a fifty-nine point four percent participation by people eligible for WIC and received a state grant of ten million six hundred fifteen, nine hundred fifty-seven dollars. The amount spent per person was one hundred four dollars and ninety-eight cents. In Vermont, the participation was seventy-six point three percent - one of the highest in the nation – and Vermont received thirteen million, forty-nine thousand, forty-two dollars, with an individual cost of one hundred sixteen dollars and seventy-eight cents. Maine had only a fifty-two percent participation rate and received a grant for seventeen million, nine hundred thirty-six thousand, six hundred thirteen dollars. The cost per individual was one hundred sixteen dollars and twenty-three cents. Certainly it seems that the benefits of the program are greater than the costs but unfortunately, all of the nutrition programs of the USDA have seen cuts in recent federal budgets.

SNAP, TEFAP, CSFP are all programs that are included in the farm bill. Also in the farm bill are the Fresh Fruit and Vegetable Program and the Senior Farmers' Market Nutrition Program. The USDA-Food and Nutrition Service also administrates the following programs that are not contained in the farm bill: WIC, NSLP, SFSP, SBP, CACFP and the Special Milk Program. Other nutrition programs come under the Older Americans Act: the Congregate Nutrition Program, the Home Delivered -Nutrition Program, Grants to Native Americans: Supportive and Nutrition Services, and the Nutrition Services Incentive Program (NSIP). A confusing mishmash of alphabet soup, eh?

The Fresh Fruit and Vegetable Program provides free fresh fruit and vegetables to children in participating elementary schools. These are served during the school day and at snack times apart from school breakfast and lunch. This program is targeted to the schools with the highest percentage of free- and reduced-cost lunch-eligible students in their enrollment and it is administered by the states. The usual supplemental food cost per child is fifty dollars to seventy-five dollars per school year.

The Special Milk Program provides milk for children in schools, child care institutions and eligible camps. Eligible to participate in the Special Milk Program are those schools and other institutions that are not receiving aid through another federal nutrition program. An exception is that schools in the School Lunch Program may participate and provide milk to eligible children in half-day programs that aren't providing lunch.

The Senior Farmers' Market Nutrition Program awards grants to states, federally-recognized tribal governments and US Territories to provide low-income seniors with coupons to use to buy fresh fruits, vegetables, honey and herbs from farm stands, farmer's markets or other community-sustained agriculture programs. It is administered by the individual states.

The Congregate Nutrition Program is familiar to most people; this is the source behind the community meals attended by seniors over the age of sixty and often, their caregivers or relatives and disabled persons. It is meant to provide a nutritious meal in a group setting to at-risk elders and to provide them with an opportunity to socialize. The program is targeted at elders in rural communities, those most at risk of being institutionalized, minority seniors, and those who are low-income and/or have difficulties with proficiency in English.

The National Survey of Older Americans Act Participants found that the majority of eaters at congregate meals were older than seventy-five years and that fifty-eight percent of these people stated that the meal would be more than one-half of their food intake for that day. Seventy-six percent of the elders said that their health had improved since they began eating at the meals and seventy-seven percent said that they are eating healthier foods since joining the congregate meal program.

Home-delivered meals are often the first interface an elderly person may have with the various elder services. The Home Delivered Nutrition Services Program authorizes meals and other nutrition services to be delivered to homebound elders. Often, a person is introduced to this service after a health crisis, at which point a referral is made by a concerned health care provider, a relative or the person himself. It targets people with the same challenges as the congregate meals program. Like the congregate meals program, most of the participants are over age seventy-five and obtain more than half of their daily food from the delivered meal. More than half of these seniors live alone and ninety-one percent of them state that the home-delivered meals have enabled them to remain in their own homes and not be institutionalized. An often unspoken additional benefit of the program is that the delivery is also a safety check. If there is anything unusual or alarming at the recipient's home, the delivery person will contact the appropriate person or agency to help the elder, for example, an ambulance if the elder is unresponsive or has fallen. Our friend Al, who was a volunteer driver for many years, became fond of the clients to whom he delivered and said that he always checked to be sure the person was okay and would chat a little with them. He said that many of the clients looked forward just to seeing someone to whom they could complain about the weather or their current aches and pains. Three times during his volunteer years, he found a client needing ambulance services.

Nutrition and supportive services are available through grants to federally recognized Native American tribal governments. These services are administered by the tribal governments involved and provide services to elders in their homes and in the community. They also provide caregiver support services and nutrition education for caregivers. I ate lunch at a meal for elders when I was working as a physician on a very remote Navajo reservation. The nearest full-service supermarket was sixty miles away. I was age-eligible for the meal, but certainly wasn't as nutrition-challenged as the other elders. After all, I was employed and had transportation.

The Nutrition Services Incentive Program purchases USDA commodity foods to supply to states and tribes that efficiently supply nutritious meals to seniors, providing an incentive to these states and tribes to provide more meals assistance to elders.

PART TWO

Misperceptions

The Deadbeats and Welfare Moms

Whenever I talked with my friend Val about this book project, she would get very upset. She is most critical and skeptical about whether food program recipients really deserve the help. "Why can't people just pull in their belts a bit. I came to this country as an immigrant, and we had very little money, but we just made do and got by."

Val is remembering a different time. Today, the hungry are working – in about fifty-six percent of the hungry households, at least one member has been working in the past year, or is currently working. Thirty-eight percent of these people have been working full-time. Even so, eighty-nine percent of the families utilizing supplemental food programs have an annual income of thirty thousand dollars or less. The belt has run out of holes to pull tighter.

Approximately one half of the clients of feeding programs in northern New England are of working age. Children make up about thirty percent and elders sixteen percent. However, the increase in need is greatest among children and seniors, and with the retirement of baby boomers, is projected to further increase among seniors.

You have now met Colleen, a young woman who is about the age that Val remembers herself when she was "pulling in her belt." You have also seen Colleen's budget, based on her fulltime employment as a medical assistant. She has studied hard and is qualified as a physical therapy assistant and had hopes for a good job in that field. The reality is that there are jobs, but only part-time positions, without benefits, and that would leave her even worse off than she is. Colleen is representative of more than half of the clients of food programs who are working poor. Like most of the people who are working hard for marginal wages, Colleen knows that she has to have nutritious food in order to be able to work and to keep herself well and functioning. She is young and most of the time, she is able to remain hopeful that she will find a full-time job in physical therapy and that she will still enjoy a satisfying and productive working life, but there are days when all that's left in her cupboard is a partial loaf of bread and a jar of peanut butter. On those days, Colleen sees only a life of lonely deprivation and desperation.

Judy is another hard worker who seems to have reached the end of her employability because kids are being hired for the low-paying jobs that she's held during most of her working life. At forty-five, employers might interview her, but they don't call her back. Judy visits food programs in order to feed her family. This is now her job – to scrounge for food to feed her children. She is bone-tired and looks it. She is proud to point out that her kids have stayed in school and the eldest is now enrolled at community college on a scholarship. Judy sees opportunities for her children as very narrow, but encourages them to get all the education they can.

Suzy is a good example of the large percentage of the hungry who are disabled (fifty-five percent in NH, fifty-seven percent in Vermont and thirty-eight percent in Maine). As you've seen, Suzy is very well-educated and has enjoyed a fulfilling and respected professional career. Now she is diminished by her illness and needs the charity of others. She feels this deeply, but guards her dignity by not allowing the experience to embitter her. Suzy is an exceptional manager of her meager finances and of the food she receives and she manages to give back by volunteering her time whenever she is able. Somehow, she continues to view her glass as half full and to be deeply grateful for the gift of food from others. Her photo album of bouquets donated by Trader Joe's is balm for her soul.

About thirty percent of the hungry in northern New England are children. You've met Ethan and have had a peek into a life that is definitely not storybook pretty. In his case, and that of many other children, his hunger results from his parents' fecklessness, substance abuse, illness or other misfortune. The point is that it is not the fault of the child but both he and society lose because his malnutrition adversely affects his school performance and his health, costing us money in illness visits to urgent care centers, emergency rooms or doctors' offices and costing us in terms of unrealized potential in a future economic situation. This is why there are more federally funded programs available for children, but these are under-utilized because of issues such as lack of local sponsors/administrators and/or transportation. In fact, in too many areas, people don't even know these programs are available.

Ellen is a good representative of the fastest growing group among the hungry – the seniors or elders. As we've seen, Ellen and her husband did everything they could to prepare for a fulfilling retirement, only to have illness and her husband's need for nursing home care prior to his death reduce Ellen to being essentially homeless (thankfully she has a very caring daughter, but what about the Ellens who have no children?) and losing her independence. At the moment, seniors make up about sixteen percent of the hungry in our region, but they also are the fastest growing group of marginalized people in our American society.

Why is this? Many of today's seniors initially had some sort of pension plan associated with their work but with the restructuring of many companies to do away with pensions or the loss of capital in 401 (k) plans or personal IRAs during the Great Recession, most have lost much, if not all, of their retirement savings.

"Too frail to work, too poor to retire will become the new "normal" for many elderly Americans," writes Edward Siedle in Forbes magazine, as he writes about the fate of the Baby Boomers. Contrary to what the financial industry would have you believe, independent experts, such as Siedle and Theresa Ghilarducci of the New School for Economic Research, estimate that the average balance held in 401(k) plans by sixty-five year old workers today is twenty-five thousand dollars. That won't buy many bags of groceries. Lulu has also found that her "golden years" are not going to be easy or comfortable. She will have to re-apply regularly for the various assistance programs for which she's eligible and will suffer the silent shame of feeling that she is no longer a valued member of society . . . even though she has contributed for more than forty-five years to that same society. Currently, she is awaiting placement in senior subsidized housing.

OK, what about the "welfare moms" – this is the stereotype of the young woman who makes a "career" of making babies and living on public assistance. The statistics demonstrate that most of the people receiving food aid are working or have recently worked. . . or they are necessary caretakers for others. The "welfare-to-work" program is training many young mothers to enter or re-enter the workforce with enhanced skills. Also, who is the single mom? The National Longitudinal Survey of Youth, which began interviewing thousands of young Americans annually in 1997, has found that forty-seven percent of all births are out of wedlock and that the millennial generation regards this as the norm. In fact, seventy-four percent of women who did not have at least a bachelor's degree had at least one child without being married. Many of these babies (twenty-eight percent) were born into unmarried partnerships, which may or may not be less stable than marriages, especially when one considers the current (2014) divorce rate of fifty percent. Raising a child alone does seriously limit one's earning ability – day care is expensive and good daycare is limited, wages are low and benefits mostly not available, and the killer is scheduling. Most jobs available are in low-wage occupations and most do not offer full-time hours. Women are disproportionately affected by this, especially when you factor in the latest tool used by employers: computer-generated scheduling that may break a person's daily eight hours into several chunks, separated by intervals of several hours. This wreaks havoc on childcare, working a second job, arranging appointments for healthcare and on life in general. It is convenient and probably cost-effective for employers because it matches the number of people working to the flow of customers at a particular time of day. This type of scheduling is especially prevalent in the fast food and retail industries.

Having said this, let me remind you that the largest percentage of people using food programs (and by definition, eligible to do so) are the working poor and most of them have worked within the past year – about forty percent of them full-time. So unemployed single moms make up a small percentage of those utilizing food programs and are probably included in the small percentage listed as "caretaker/other." According to the Council on Contemporary Families, fifteen point two million children live in poverty with their married parents; sixteen point seven million children live in poverty with one parent. And make no mistake: single parenting is equally difficult for a father as it is for a mother.

Each food program serves some households that are chronically poor. The chronically poor are people who know no other way to survive but using the social welfare system as a surrogate parent to care for them. These are a small percentage of the overall population using the food programs.

And yes, there are alcoholics and drug users who come to food programs, but the percentage is probably equal to the prevalence in the general population – eight percent according to the National Council on Alcoholism and Drug Dependence, Inc. It is higher among the homeless, who make up less than five percent of the people served by these food programs (obviously more of the homeless use the communal meals than the pantry programs.) However, the need for sustenance is not reserved for the healthy, upright and righteous among us – we all need to eat. Why and how a person became dependent on alcohol or drugs has nothing to do with his basic need for food, but has everything to do with how quickly their health declines from the ravages of substance abuse.

Anyone can walk in and get free food. Yes, anyone can eat at the communal meals. Many settings, like the Senior Meals, will ask a donation of one to three dollars per meal, but will not turn away those people who can't pay. These programs have a dual purpose: feeding the hungry and providing socialization for people who might otherwise be isolated and become emotionally ill. It also serves as a check-up to make sure that marginalized elders or disabled people are well and safe. If Margie is having more balance problems, or Joe can't remember where he lives, a volunteer or concerned neighbor will help to direct them to pertinent services. . . or more to the point, direct services to Margie or Joe.

All of the pantry programs (those that distribute free groceries) have eligibility requirements that have been established by the USDA (US Department of Agriculture). These requirements are checked at a person's first visit to a pantry and then at least yearly. The USDA has established an eligibility of one hundred thirty percent of the Federal poverty level [see Appendix A] to determine eligibility for commodity food distributed through food programs by the USDA and most food pantries use this to determine income eligibility. Some programs also require proof of residence in the particular community or state.

As you can see from Appendix B the eligibility requirements to obtain SNAP (food stamp) benefits is rigorous and requires multiple pieces of documentation. This, plus pride, is probably why only about one third of eligible seniors use the program.

Some pantry programs require proof of residency – either in the community or in the state. Those that are specific about state residency are usually in areas bordering other states. A few programs are run by town governments specifically for the residents of those towns.

Food programs provide unhealthy food. In fact, most food programs are very mindful of trying to provide healthy choices for their patrons. They are constrained by the same considerations as most of us: price, availability and in their case, the additional constraint of what has been donated. I've "shopped" at the VT Food Bank with Lisa Pitcher of Our Place Drop-In Center and watched how she chose her purchases. She chose crates of apples, a huge package of carrots, crates of cauliflower and banana boxes (the standard packing box of food programs) of low-salt canned tomatoes, canned peas, soups and other vegetables. She picked up several boxes of low-salt, low-fat chicken broth for use in their lunch program and several "treats" like cereals from the "free" (donated) food. She also chose a carton of individually boxed juices for the children. The day we visited, there was a windfall of donated frozen meat, but it would not be available for distribution until the next day (all donations have to be inspected to be sure they meet safety requirements). All of the programs I've visited try to provide each household with eggs – a half-dozen to a dozen – but are struggling with the current high price of eggs. Milk and yoghurt are also items that often have to be purchased by pantries.

The emphasis when stocking the food pantries is on vegetables, either fresh or canned, protein sources, preferably frozen donations or beans or peanut butter, and whole grain breads and pastas. Cereals provided are low-sugar whole grain choices like Cheerios. Check out the WIC eligible foods in Appendix C.

There's just not enough food. I've heard several people say that hunger exists because there is not enough food being produced and then pointing to such things as the egg shortage because of disease in chickens. In fact, in the US, thirty to forty percent of all food is wasted. This is equal to twenty pounds of food per person per month. Or about seventy billion tons lost for human consumption. Because the rotting food in landfills adds to the burden of greenhouse gasses affecting our atmosphere and thereby, to global warming, this is also environmentally unviable. In answer to these concerns, four New England states (CT, MA, RI, VT) have passed mandatory food waste recycling laws, with Vermont's Universal Recycling Act requiring any business producing one hundred four tons or more of food waste to first) donate edible food to food programs for human consumption, second), food not deemed edible by humans, but not rotting, to be donated to farms for animal consumption and third) the rest to be composted.

They (food stamp recipients) just sell their debit cards to buy drugs and alcohol. Since most of the recipients of food stamp benefits are the families of the working poor and increasingly, the elderly, it is unlikely that substance abuse is any higher in this group than in the general population. This is an assumption, but it is fact that Food Stamp fraud of any type accounts for only one to two percent of the SNAP program monies distributed.

Food programs don't help get rid of hunger. Many people have told me the adage about giving a man a fish only feeds him that day, but teaching him to fish will feed him in the future and this is true. However, it is also true that human beings, be they children, working adults or seniors, need to eat every day and learning and marketing skills doesn't happen in a day. Many of the food programs are trying to address longer terms goals through culinary programs, basic employment skill training, resume classes and other similar small programs. Food programs cannot solve all of our social problems; they exist to feed our hungry.

The Feeding America 2014 study indicated that forty percent of agencies (pantries & communal meals) provided educational services related to SNAP application (food stamps) and more than one-third of agencies help clients with non-food needs, such as budgeting, time-management, etc.

All the funding for food programs comes from my taxes. In fact, almost all of the money is donated by individuals, corporations or charitable trusts. The Federal government funds SNAP (the food stamp program), and the programs discussed in part I, but the amount is small. Only one point eighteen percent of the total federal budget goes to food and agriculture combined.

So What if She's Hungry? What's It to Me?

It is easier to ignore hunger when we don't think we know anyone who's hungry and when we think that someone else's hunger has no practical implication for us. Since fourteen point three percent of households in the United States have a problem of too little food, it is probable that each of us knows (or is related to) at least one individual who is hungry. As we've seen with Colleen and Suzy, these are sometimes surprising people – educated, working, well-dressed – and they live in our neighborhoods. This is true unless you are one of the isolated privileged people who never rub elbows with the hoi polloi.

Actually, let's talk for a moment or two about the privileged. We have a great divide – a Grand Canyon – in our society today and the split widens daily. In fact, in 2015, the widening disparity between haves and have nots is greatest in New Hampshire, as reported in New Hampshire Business Review. It is easy to fall into stereotyping the privileged just as many sterotype the needy, styling the privileged as greedy, selfish people who turn their backs on those less fortunate. I think that this is mostly untrue, just as seeing the hungry as deadbeats is untrue.

We have in our society been gradually separated into enclaves of those who have and those who don't and each group is increasingly invisible to the other. Oh yes, we all know of the existence of the rich and the poor, but mostly we think of the group to which we don't belong as an amorphous mass, not as living breathing human beings who bleed when cut and who agonize over the illnesses and hurts of their loved ones. Inequality in a society does this to us: it makes the poles of our society strangers to one another.

Today, many privileged people have relatives that qualify as downwardly mobile and verging on poverty, but as long as these relatives observe the convention of wearing decent clothing and remaining discreet about their circumstances, the family dynamic gives power and gratitude to the bountiful father/brother/daughter/sister who picks up the tab at family outings. One doesn't inquire too deeply about the circumstances of the sibling who has frayed cuffs or wears the same dress for all of the occasions. There is embarrassment in our society about not being affluent. It may have roots in our Puritan traditions and in the immigrant ambition to rise on the socio-economic scale, but whatever it is, we don't want people to know that we're slipping into poverty. We feel a deep sense of failure and a lack of validation as worthy citizens and family members. It is profoundly shaming to almost anyone who doesn't have the acceptable excuse of illness and even to some who do – "it's my fault I'm sick. . . lame. . . depressed." We left behind the tugging of forelocks generations ago and we've been acculturated to expect that we will be the masters of our own destinies; it is a very humbling experience to find that many other factors impact us.

What has happened? Since 2007, there has been erosion of the middle class – both in income and in wealth as measured by savings or real estate – and an increase in the wealth of the top earners. I'm not just talking about the much-discussed 1%, but also perhaps the one percent in each age group. For example, Kyle, who was thirty and earning one hundred thirty thousand dollars per year in 2010, was among the top one percent of wage earners in his age group. To remain in that category when he is thirty-five, he will need an income of two hundred ten thousand dollars and he is on track to be earning this much. This is much less than people are used to thinking – I know several doctors, dentists and lawyers who earn in excess of two hundred fifty thousand dollars per year, but who maintain that they are not privileged. "I'm just a middle-class working stiff like anyone else." But are they?

Most of us look to those above us to gauge our ranking in the pecking order. The engineer earning a quarter million dollars per year feels like he's small change compared with his boss who earns half a million. To say that he is one of the privileged is usually denied because he still falls short of the greatest wealth.

The big difference between these high wage earners and the marginalized people at or just above minimum wage is that the high earner buys what he wants for dinner, not what he can afford. He also is able to buy new clothes, a nice home and then to sock away a nice nest egg toward retirement or following an avocation. The marginalized person has no extra left over for savings; she puts all of her money back into the general economy. She works just as hard or harder as a licensed nursing assistant as does the doctor in the same hospital, but enjoys none of the security. The patient in the bed is reliant on her care for his comfort and safety for each of her twelve-hour shifts. This is not minimizing the importance of the doctor's training, knowledge and ability to diagnose and prescribe treatment, but the importance of the person who actually gives the hour-to-hour care must also not be denigrated.

My use of gender above is deliberate: only eleven percent of the one percent are women.

It is also important to realize that the privileged accrue wealth, either through simple compound interest or by investments. So after a certain point, they are made wealthy by their money with little further effort or expertise being necessary. The marginalized person damages her health and further earning power by the constant effort and anxiety necessary to simply maintain her fragile status quo.

Being privileged is an isolating condition. It usually implies moving upward in the housing market and living in splendid seclusion or in enclaves of similarly monied people. One loses touch with less wealthy friends and family because the less wealthy can't keep up with the costly recreation and entertainment – not to mention dining – enjoyed by the privileged and tend to drop off contact. Unless the privileged person is footing the bill and that changes the dynamic of the relationship irretrievably.

This relative isolation ensures that someone like Kyle has no appreciation of the life of a person working at the check-out counter in the upscale market in his town, let alone the pizza delivery guy or the laundress who does his shirts. He just thinks they are not able to buy luxury goods, not that they might be skipping meals in order to feed their kids or not buying needed medicines in order to buy food. His lack of compassion is situational and one could say an educational deficit, in that he's uneducated about the plight of fourteen point seven percent of American people with whom he feels little or no commonality.

In the meantime, the middle class is shrinking and as much as twenty-five percent of our population is hovering on the line between middle class and poor. This is due to the changed labor market and to the great losses suffered by the Baby Boomers in the Great Recession. The irony is that in the developing world the middle class is growing exponentially, with India having the largest middle class in the world right now.

The US ranks fourth among one hundred forty-one countries for income inequality; only Russia, Ukraine and Lebanon have greater inequality. Do we admire the economies of these countries? Do we consider them stable?

Economists, including several Nobel laureates, consider our economy to be endangered by the high and growing degree of inequality. They point out that this causes stagnation in an economy, when the middle class shrinks and the middle and lower classes cannot support the growth of the economy by buying that country's goods and services. (This is why economists consider food stamps a good deal; food stamps put one dollar seventy-three cents back into the economy for every one dollar dispersed.) There is good cause for alarm because the "recovery" from the Great Recession of 2008 has not led to an increase in wages and the jobs increase has been primarily in low-wage, part-time jobs. In actuality, the differential is even greater when non-wage compensation, such as health insurance, paid sick days, etc. is factored in.

The expert economists are worried about the "economy" and what it means for us as a strong nation and a world power. What happens to the hungry is a matter of statistics and the statistics indicate that we are in trouble and there is a crisis brewing. If one looks at history, it is clear that a society with such inequality as we have today in this country is very unstable. People can be used and abused only so long before they revolt. Let us be instrumental in making sure that a political revolution occurs, not a bloody one or an implosion, such as Russia saw.

As you've learned, all of the food programs are charitable efforts and rely on donations, both of food and of money. Even Feeding America, which supplies food and services to all of the contiguous US, is dependent on the generosity of donors. Knowing this led me to ask, "who are the donors?" It is intuitive to think that the bulk of donations come from those who have the most: the wealthy and privileged. Is this so?

Individuals contribute seventy-two percent of overall charitable giving, according to Giving USA Foundation. Based on itemized tax returns, individuals whose income is one hundred thousand dollars or less give the most – three point six percent of their income, and individuals at the highest end (over two hundred thousand), give three point one percent of their income. Giving by those whose income is between one hundred thousand and two hundred thousand is two point six percent.

I was especially interested in where each group donates – to charities that help people with basic human needs, such as food, clothing and shelter versus such visible things as endowing buildings at universities or medical centers, being named supporters of the arts, etc. Nothing wrong with any of these causes and interests and they all enrich us, but I think that looking at where we put our 'disposable' money is an indicator of what slice of American life is visible to us.

This chart summarizes what I learned:

Household Income	% who contribute to meet basic needs	Average amount given to meet basic needs	% of household giving donated to meet basic needs
<$100,000	25.8%	$365	45.1%
$100K - $200K	46.2%	$657	12.9%
$200 K – 1 Million	74.5%	$3,076	22.9%
>$1 Million	76.4%	$12,673	10.2%

Data from the Center on Philanthropy at Indiana University

To me, this clearly illustrates the point made earlier that as we become more affluent, the poor become less visible to us. It is like climbing a real ladder: we rarely look down – our eyes are glued to the feet of the one above us and when we do look, it's up, not down. So it is with the socioeconomic ladder.

Another reason that hunger matters to each of us – beyond the moral imperative – is that chronically undernourished people do not have good health. As a practicing physician for more than forty years, I have observed this myself. The poor health of the underprivileged (read uninsured or underinsured as well as malnourished) is a drain on all of us and yes, this involves public monies, either through Medicaid or through higher hospital and doctors' bills as the cost of keeping the poor alive is passed on to those of us who are marginally more fortunate. This pass-on is through our taxes directly or through the inflated costs we pay for our medical care. Don't for a minute think that it's fairly apportioned – those who have no insurance or those who are underinsured pay the highest freight.

The most fragile groups, the children and the elderly, are the most at risk for the health problems that follow hunger. Children who are malnourished don't have the resources to fight off infectious diseases and are more often sick and more often end up in the hospital. The lack of nutrients also affects their developing minds in a variety of ways, leading to poorer school performance and a loss of potential. This costs us in several ways: the additional cost of schooling to try to bring children up to grade level and the cost in lost potential as these children progress through school unable to apply themselves and attain the skills necessary for a rewarding and fulfilling vocation after school. We need their skills and we need their natural aptitudes to be developed so that we, the American society, can benefit from their contributions.

Another alarming trend is the rise in obesity and type 2 diabetes in our children. This was virtually unheard of when I was a young doctor; now it is common. While there are other complicating factors in individual cases, much of this is due to diets high in simple carbohydrates (read "starches") and fat found in the fast foods and affordable choices of poor families. And yes, we are seeing these problems in adults of all ages. It is very expensive to maintain reasonable health for a diabetic, especially when one factors in time lost from work and the stress on a family. Much of this cost ends up transmitted to the larger society.

Our malnourished elders are facing the same health challenges and for them it means frequent visits for medical care and when diabetes and/or high blood pressure are the culprits, often end-stage renal disease results. What many people don't know is that end-stage renal disease is a very special category for Medicare coverage and it is completely covered. This, plus the increase in illness due to high blood pressure and diabetes secondary to obesity have led to the increased need for dialysis centers. If you want an index of how healthy we all are, look around your community and see how far it is to the nearest dialysis center. As recently as twenty-five years ago, people had to travel to larger medical centers to have dialysis. . . and rural areas usually had one centrally located one. Now there is often more than one center in any town of ten to fifteen thousand. And your tax dollars pay for a lot of it. No, I'm not arguing that we shouldn't spend our money to treat end-stage renal disease, but I do think we need to make the link with unhealthy lifestyle and how helping our less privileged to enjoy healthier dietary choices will save money for all of us.

Abundant and nutritious food is vital to each senior in order that she be able to be independent as long as possible. Falls are often the beginning of the end for the elderly and when one is malnourished, balance is not good, nor is the ability to mend bones or heal torn skin. Confusion also results from chronic malnutrition and various vitamin deficiencies. Communities are healthier and more vibrant when they are made up of active residents of all ages and certainly our healthcare costs are driven up by the costs of ailing elders. Let's prevent this to the best of our abilities.

Education

Privileged young people like Kyle tend to come from solidly middle or upper class families, brought up in stable households where both parents are present and are also well-educated. The rags-to-riches stories of our parents' and grandparents' generations are now rare. For example, Ethan will need to have an unbroken string of good luck from now on to compensate for his marginalized beginnings in order to have a shot at a college education and a materially comfortable future. Unfortunately, that it how it is today and the American Dream is only available to the few.

One of the key elements necessary to rising from food insecurity and a marginalized position in our society is education. Although we have free public education, many kids today are passed through school without learning to properly read: they are functionally illiterate. Much is written about the schools and how to reform education, and there are some promising beginnings in many areas. One thing that I think is overlooked and that has been bred by our pop psychology concern with children's self-esteem is that praising children for simply doing what is expected is not healthy and does not raise self-esteem. It simply implies that very little is expected and that the child can expect praise, promotion and the whole bag of goodies through life just for showing up. Examples are kindergarten 'graduation', social promotion from one grade to the next and in college, the awarding of a passing grade based solely on attendance. These do not teach the value of work or teach good learning habits; they teach kids that they are entitled to the benefits of schooling or work or whatever, without putting in effort. The result is not self-esteem.

We also fail our kids by not teaching them the basics of personal finance. I'm not talking about economic theory or how to make a killing in the stock market or how to leverage a hostile takeover of a company. No, I'm talking about how to make a budget, balance a checkbook or use personal finance software, how to prepare your taxes and even how to grocery shop and make frugal, but nutritious choices.

Brittany is a bright young mother who was enrolled in my friend's licensed nursing assistant class as a welfare-to-work student. Brittany had become pregnant when she was just out of high school and although her parents were able to help her through her pregnancy, they are not in a position to help her raise her daughter. Brittany graduated in the upper decile of her class and was planning to study to be a paralegal. Today, she has trouble finding gas money to get to class at the end of each month. She has a clear record of end-of-month absences. Her assessment is that she just doesn't get enough money, but during the first three weeks of the month, she shows up at class with a large designer coffee each day, keeps a pack of cigarettes handy for the breaks and has the latest i-phone. My friend tried to counsel Brittany that if she made coffee at home, quit smoking and perhaps used the messaging plan on her phone less, she'd probably make it through the month, maybe with money to spare. This is absolutely foreign thinking to Brittany – "everyone else" can go to Starbucks and "everyone else" that she knows smokes and she just *has* to message her friends. . . why should she be different? Brittany is an individual, but her circumstances are very similar to many of the young women participating in the welfare-to-work programs. It is easy to criticize them and denigrate their families, but it would be more productive to look at how we have failed them.

We cannot assume that young people receive a proper education about handling finances at home. According to the Pew Charitable Trusts, roughly seventy percent of households in the US today face serious savings, income or debt problems. Some of this is due to the new realities of our national economy: stagnation of wages, shift from a majority of new jobs being full-time to now being part-time without benefits, and fully one quarter of jobs that are now low-wage. Also, fifty-five percent of households do not have sufficient savings to sustain them through an emergency; almost half of households are spending everything they earn or going into debt. Fourteen point seven percent of the households are at poverty level and fifty-six percent have poor credit. Clearly, societal change is imperative, but so is teaching people to better manage the resources that they do have.

In this milieu of entitlement in which each young person should have at least an i-phone with a generous airtime plan and a car – preferably decent-looking – and funds for 'fun' and music, the least we owe ourselves (who eventually pick up the tab, either as parents or as a society) is to educate our students on how to manage their money. I believe we should have a mandatory course for high school freshmen or sophomores that includes all of the financial tools that these young people will need to stretch whatever money they earn/receive as far as possible. And they should learn the very basic fact that credit cards are not a solution to the problem of too little money.

In several of the food programs that I visited, savvy volunteers help recipients learn to manage their money more effectively, especially those who are in need, but don't qualify for monthly food aid. At the Community Kitchen in Keene, NH someone suggested pairing elders, who were hungry because a) they had outlived their resources, b) had lost their nest egg in the stock market downturn, c) had some disaster that ate all of their savings, with younger recipients. It was hoped that the elders could teach the younger recipients how to better manage what they did have, both in budgeting money and in planning food use.

In helping people learn to manage wisely, there are resources in each community that can be utilized, including bankers who would be happy to speak about using bank products such as checking and savings accounts, grocery stores that would accommodate "how to shop" tours, debt specialists who can elucidate the perils of credit and many others. These are valid areas of community service and would enrich us all.

Senior Storm

We are an aging nation and very alarming trends now face our elders. Right now, more than ten million seniors in this wealthy country are hungry. These are the same people who raised many of us and who clucked over whether or not we cleaned our plates. The plates filled by their labor. Now, their plates are empty. . . and some of them are homeless.

What has happened? It is always easy to blame people for their misfortune and many seniors do blame themselves. Many of the baby boomers, who are now retiring, lost pensions through company bankruptcies, restructuring and all the other terms that mean the employee is paying for the mismanagement of company executives. My friend Bee, a widow, thought her retirement was taken care of by her late husband's pension from United Airlines. Wrong! United Airlines managed to walk away from a restructuring owing its pensioned employees only pennies on the dollar. This or similar scenarios have happened to many people who are now sixty plus. Next came the Great Recession and many of the same people lost most of the retirement monies that they had invested in private portfolios or mutual funds, in IRAs or 401 (k)s. That was depressing enough, but what really compounds it (pun intended) is that the Federal Reserve has kept interest rates low to help the economy rebound. This means that bank interest and the interest earnings on bonds has also stayed low. So, not only do we, the elders, not have enough time to see our money grow again, that same money earns little through compounding.

Of course, I haven't even mentioned the number of people who lost their jobs in the economic downturn – many were in their prime earning years but also past prime as far as hiring goes. So mid-level managers have had to take low-wage, part-time jobs because nothing else is available to them. A high-level executive laid off from McDonald's now works in an Amazon warehouse in AZ, loading boxes.

This former McDonald's executive is not the only senior working at Amazon's warehouses. A phenomenon of elderly migrant workers has appeared here in the land of opportunity. Many elderly Americans are traveling the US highways in RVs, working at low-wage or craft-type jobs and following the seasons to avoid heating costs. A "town" has grown up around a particular enclave of battered old RVs in AZ. The nucleus for this town is the Amazon warehouse where many residents work long shifts, packing and loading goods for shipment to Amazon customers. Most of the residents had decent jobs and full lives prior to some economic or medical event that caused them to lose most of their assets. Many have now spent their health on this low-wage, physically brutal work.

John and Nancy are in their late sixties and have raised and educated four children. Five years ago, just after John retired, Nancy became ill and required lengthy and expensive hospitalization. Their insurance covered eighty percent of the costs but the remainder was disastrous for the couple. John took a reverse mortgage on their home to pay the medical bills. Nancy recovered, but their financial circumstances worsened by the month. The mortgage payment left them with too little money to pay the other bills and eventually, they defaulted. Now John and Nancy are essentially homeless. None of their children is in a position to support them in independent living, so they "visit" each child for monthly periods. It's a solution, but one that none of them foresaw happening.

Experts have said that each person who is now between sixty and ninety can expect one year of food insecurity in her remaining life. And it is projected that by 2025, fully half of the hungry will be seniors. This is partly due to the increasing numbers of seniors as Baby Boomers retire and partly to the worsening economic status of seniors.

There are changes afoot that will help the working poor and their families, such as a rise in the minimum wage, but these will not help the elderly. Nothing is being discussed that will help the generation that has worked so hard not only to raise their own families, but also to make many of the inventions, innovations and contributions to industry, commerce, medicine, and the arts that have made life better for so many Americans. Is this generation (my generation) condemned to live on charity?

Right now, ten million seniors are known to have too little to eat. They have to choose daily whether to eat or buy medicine, eat or buy heating fuel. Only one-third of the eligible seniors apply for food stamps. This is partly because many can't quite believe that they are eligible, or they are too embarrassed by their need. After all, it wasn't that long ago that they were the ones giving to all of the charities. It is so humiliating to not be able to provide one's own basic needs.

Many seniors don't know how or where to apply for food stamps or to access other programs. Small rural towns don't often have true senior centers or newspapers and many individuals have become isolated through their lack of funds for socializing. Seniors are less likely than other age groups to have previously utilized SNAP or other benefit programs and have little personal knowledge of them. When the current generation of seniors was young, jobs were more plentiful and the wages were adequate to supporting a family, so applying for aid carries the stigma of not being able to do your part or to provide for your own. Unfortunately, even the proudest and previously independent senior needs to eat and have basic needs met. Not only do seniors stress about being seen entering a social services office, they stress about the scorn of the person at the check-out in the grocery store. Seventy-six percent of seniors feel stigma attached to food stamps, compared to sixty percent of younger people.

Another issue is transportation. In our rural areas, with little public transportation, our elders become increasingly dependent on others. Medical issues can precipitate the loss of a driving license or a vehicle and suddenly, there is no way to shop, see the doctor, or pick up a prescription. Equally, there is no way to go to apply for aid. It also doesn't help many seniors to be able to file paperwork online. An economically marginalized elder will not usually have Internet access. For many seniors, the jargon of applying for aid is like a foreign language. All of these are barriers to our elders – our parents, grandparents, favorite aunt or uncle – receiving aid they badly need.

Remember Lulu? Like most seniors, Lulu has worked and contributed to society and her own community all of her adult life. Now she suddenly has no money and no way to earn more. Maybe she made a few less wise decisions, but who among us hasn't? Mostly she's been a productive and frugal person but she didn't have the opportunity to make up what she lost in the Great Recession nor the health and skills to compete in the new economy. She is one of many seniors in the same predicament. So are John and Nancy. And so may I be . . . or you. We are each one medical disaster, one fire, one flood, one robbery, one identity theft. . .you name it. . . away from being hungry.

Hope

As my husband and I wound up our year of visiting food programs, I felt as though I was Scrooge, looking through a glass at Christmas Future, and the aspect was not good. I saw my peers, the elders, cold and hungry and wondering what had all our hard work profited us. I saw more children raiding dumpsters for food discarded by the privileged. I saw more parents unable to supervise their children because each parent had to work two or three jobs, just to keep the family housed, clothed and fed. I saw a greater disconnect between those who have and those who do not, and greater numbers in the latter category. For a brief while, I despaired and panicked at this glimpse of the near future.

Hope began to poke its green bud when I thought of the efforts and compassion of all the people involved in the various food programs. . and it blossomed further when I thought of the innovative steps being taken by some to expand their programs beyond giving out emergency food. The idea of a food processing plant that would enable hungry people access to summer's bounty all year long, while also helping to support the food programs in NH, the farm programs partnering with food pantries and the growth of educational programs around food preparation, food and money management were heartening. Just the fact that some people involved in feeding the hungry have vision and aspirations for the future of the hungry, i.e., to come closer to solving the problem of hunger, is uplifting.

I hope that we will pass a higher minimum wage sufficient to enable every person who is working to feed and care for themselves and every working household to be self-sustaining. Actually, what I really hope for is a living wage that allows families time to be together and to nourish the intellects and dreams of their children and to cherish each other.

I hope for some relief for the elders who saw their life savings and their dreams of some comfort in their "golden years" go up in the smoke of the "banks too big to fail." I hope for a solution that leaves us elders with our dignity. We worked very hard and we gave and gave and gave in hopes that the world would be better for the next generation. Well, it isn't. We failed. I hope that we as a citizenry can find the will to make it better. A solution that I see as possible and plausible is to simply extend SNAP benefits to each senior receiving less than a living threshold amount in Social Security benefits. Then each elder could eat without having to grovel or be humiliated. Surely we've at least earned this. Especially since SNAP benefits return to the greater economy almost doubled.

I hope for a minimum income. Switzerland has been playing with this idea in recent years because, ultimately, it would be better for the nation's total economy to have basic economic security enjoyed by each person. Poverty is costly to a society.

I hope for a universal single-payer health care system, with perhaps a low (five dollars or less) co-pay for services, and no further hidden costs, like the present eighty percent/twenty percent insurance most people have (can afford). Yes, our taxes would be higher, but not our actual costs and not only would we be receiving necessary services in return but no one would have to fear bankruptcy and homelessness because of illness in the family. We as a society are better people than this and it works in other countries.

I hope for a revised and progressive tax code that will enable each person to figure her own taxes and will ensure that all in this country pay his fair share. This alone should enable us to afford my wish list and keep all of us fed, housed and clothed.

I hope for an educated youth who understand personal finances and who can see when the emperor has no clothes. I hope for public education to again excel in all states and communities. The Ethans we love should have equal opportunity to the Kyles and to the children of the super wealthy. And the children of the super wealthy should have more interface with other children than simply setting aside their cast-offs to be given to the "poor." I hope that our public schools can help each child to maximize the talents with which he was born and to appreciate that we need the talents of all.

In short, I hope for this country to again be great in the opportunities and the caring it (we) extend to all people. We just joined with other UN nations to pledge to eradicate extreme poverty in the world, but there is a great deal we need to do at home.

Finally, I hope that this book has informed and inspired you. Knowledge is powerful and I believe that if we each knew of the plight of our neighbors, we would contribute our particular talents to bettering our society. The cliché about ripples in a pond is true – no matter how small the pebble you throw, the ripples spread beyond your reach.

APPENDICES

Appendix A

2014 Federal Poverty Guidelines for 48 contiguous states

Persons in household	Poverty threshold
1	$11,670
2	$15,730
3	$19,790
4	$23,850
5	$27,910
6	$31,970
7	$36,030
8	$40,090
For each additional person, add	$4,060

Source: usda.gov

Appendix B

Required Documentation for Food Stamps (~~Vermont 3Squares~~)

All of the documentation below is required before a person can receive SNAP benefits: Identification (licenses, government identification, birth certificates) and social security numbers for all members applying for assistance. A photo ID is preferred, but not required.

- All gross wages received by the applicant family in the 30 days before their application. Pay stubs or written statements from employers. Verifiable pay dates, pay frequency, hourly rate or salary and gross wages for each pay date.

- If self-employed, most recent federal income tax return including all W2s, forms, and schedules or record books showing income and expenses for the last 12 months or since the business started, whichever is less.

- Written statement from any person paying the applicant for room, room and meals, or only meals.

- Income applicant receives from providing dependent care to children or adults in their home (self-employment records or statement from person paying). Also note the number of snacks, and the number and type of meals applicant provides unless they receive reimbursement for them.

- Gross unearned income such as social security, SSI, veteran's benefits, unemployment or worker's compensation, pensions, dividends, or child support (award letter, divorce/separation papers or statement from person paying support, 1099).

- Amount of room only, meals only, or room and meals that applicant pays.

- Dependent care expenses applicant paid in the last calendar month.

- Alimony or child support payments applicant made to anyone outside their household (court order, and cancelled checks or statement from the person receiving payment).

- Savings, checking, credit union account numbers or statements of all accounts, including children's accounts,

- IRAs and profit sharing accounts.

- Rent receipt, lot rent receipt, rent lease agreement.

- Proof of mortgage payment such as cancelled check, payment book or payment schedule.

- Property tax bill and home insurance premium including the breakdown between property, contents, liability.

- Other – verification of any other information applicant provided on their application, recertification form, and Interim Report form.

Appendix C – WIC Foods

Maximum Monthly Allowances of Supplemental Foods for Children and Women

Foods	Children	------------------- Women -------------------		
	Food Package IV: 1 through 4 years	Food Package V: Pregnant and Partially Breastfeeding (up to 1 year postpartum)	Food Package VI: Postpartum (up to 6 months postpartum)	Food Package VII: Fully Breastfeeding (up to 1 year Post-partum)
Juice	128 fl oz	144 fl oz	96 fl oz	144 fl oz
Milk [2]	16 qt	22 qt	16 qt	24 qt
Breakfast cereal [3]	36 oz	36 oz	36 oz	36 oz
Cheese	N/A	N/A	N/A	1 lb
Eggs	1 dozen	1 dozen	1 dozen	2 dozen
Fruits & vegetables	$6.00 in cash value vouchers	$10.00 in cash value vouchers	$10.00 in cash value vouchers	$10.00 in cash value vouchers
Whole wheat bread	2 lb	1 lb	N/A	1 lb
Fish (canned) [5]	N/A	N/A	N/A	30 oz
Legumes, dry or canned and/or Peanut Butter	1 lb (64 oz canned) OR 18 oz	1 lb (64 oz canned) AND 18 oz	1 lb (64 oz canned) OR 18 oz	1 lb (64 oz canned) AND 18 oz

Source: usda.gov

[1] Refer to the regulatory requirements for the complete provisions and requirements for WIC foods.

[2] Allowable options for milk alternatives are cheese, soy beverage, and tofu.

[3] At least one half of the total number of breakfast cereals on State agency food list must be whole grain.

[4] Allowable options for whole wheat bread are whole grain bread, brown rice, bulgur, oatmeal, whole-grain barley, soft corn or whole wheat tortillas.

[5] Allowable options for canned fish are light tuna, salmon, sardines, and mackerel.

Appendix D

Food Program Comparisons

Name	Charitable Status	Pantry/ Meals	Paid Staff	Other Programs	Transition Plan	Audited Digital Database	Strong Board
Fall Mountain Food Shelf	Under Fall Mountain Friendly Meals	Pantry- Legally separate from senior meals	No	No	No	No; Currently putting this into effect	No
Feeding Hope Food Pantry	Church	Both	Yes	yes	No Formal plan	Yes	Through church
NH Food Bank	501(c)(3)	Food bank	Yes	Many	Yes	Yes	Yes
Lakes Region Food Pantry	501(c)(3)	Pantry	Yes	Thrift shop	In process	Yes	Yes

Name	Charit- able Status	Pantry/ Meals	Paid Staff	Other Programs	Trans- ition Plan	Audited Digital Database	Strong Board
Lakes Region Vineyard Church	Church	Both	No	No	Informal- Cross- training	Paper/ By church	Church Board
Salvation Army	Church	Both	Yes	Many	Yes	Yes	Salvation Army Board
Capital Region Food Program	501(c)(3)	Bulk distribution/ Holiday boxes	No	No	Yes	Yes	Yes
Henniker Food Pantry	501(c) (3)	Pantry	No	Social worker	In process	Yes	Yes
St. Thomas More	Church	Pantry	No	Dietary Intern	Yes	By church	Through Church

Name	Charit-able Status	Pantry/ Meals	Paid Staff	Other Programs	Trans-ition Plan	Audited Digital Database	Strong Board
Our Place Drop-In Center	501(c)(3)	Pantry & Communal meals	Yes	Shower, play and respite	Yes	Yes	Yes
Seacoast Family Food Pantry	501(c)(3)	Pantry	Yes	Interface with Farmers' Market	Yes	Yes	Yes
The Community Kitchen, Inc	501(c)(3)	Pantry & Communal meals	Yes	Gleaning program initiated by grant	Yes	Yes	More or less
Vermont Foodbank	501(c)(3)	Food Bank	Yes	Many	Yes	Yes	Yes
Good Shepherd Food Bank	501(c)(3)	Food Bank	Yes	Many	Yes	Yes	Yes

Resources

My greatest resources in researching this book were not in print; they were the people whose stories fill these pages and who were so incredibly generous with their time and their histories.

Articles

Bruder, Jessica. "The End of Retirement: When You Can't Afford to Stop Working." *Harper's*, August 15, 2014.

Books

Berg, Joel. *All You Can Eat: How Hungry Is America?* New York: Seven Stories Press, 2008.

Newman, Katherine S. *Falling from Grace: Downward Mobility in the Age of Affluence.* Berkeley: University of California Press, 1999.

Nez, Eric, and Raj Patel. *Food Rebellions!: Crisis and the Hunger for Justice.* Cape Town: Pambazuka Press, 2009.

Saul, Nick, and Andrea Curtis. *The Stop: How the Fight for Good Food Transformed a Community and Inspired a Movement.* Brooklyn, NY: Melville House Pub., 2013.

Shipler, David K. *The Working Poor: Invisible in America.* New York: Vintage Books, 2005.

Tanner, Michael, and Charles Hughes. "The War on Poverty Turns 50." The Cato Institute: October 30, 2014.

Websites

https://www.nationalpriorities.org/budget-basics/federal-budget-101/spending/

http://www.ers.usda.gov/topics/food-nutrition-assistance/food-security-in-the-us/measurement.aspx

http://www.feinsteinfoundation.org/About%20Us.htm

http://end68hoursofhunger.org/

https://carsey.unh.edu/publications?keyword=hunger&date%5Bmin%5D%5Bdat
e%5D=&date%5Bmax%5D%5D%5Bdate%5D=2014

http://www.motherjones.com/politics/2013/08/calculator-fast-food-worker-
income-wages-comparison

http://www.ers.usda.gov/topics/food-nutrition-assistance/food-security-in-the-
us/measurement.aspx

http://www.hungerfreevt.org/learn/what-is-the-issue

http://www.vtfoodbank.org/

http://www.vtfarmtoplate.com/plan/chapter/4-1-food-security-in-vermont

http://www.nytimes.com/2013/12/01/nyregion/older-workers-are-increasingly-
entering-fast-food-industry.html

http://www.vtfoodbank.org/About/AboutHunger/HouseholdFoodSecurity.aspx

http://www.feedingAmerica.org/hunger-in-America/impact-of-hunger/hunger-
and-poverty/hunger-and-poverty-fact-sheet.html

http://www.usinflationcalculator.com/

http://www.nh.gov/oep/data-center/census/

http://www.nal.usda.gov/fnic/pubs/learning.pdf

http://www.kidscoplatepledge.org/wp-content/uploads/2011/11/platepledge-the-
impact-of-nutrition.pdf

https://www.google.com/webhp?sourceid=chrome-
instant&ion=1&espv=2&ie=UTF-8#q=hunger%20in%20adults

http://thinkprogress.org/economy/2011/11/24/375776/food-insecurity-by-the-
numbers/

http://usatoday30.usatoday.com/news/health/2009-08-23-dialysis_N.htm

http://www.people-press.org/2015/01/08/the politics-of-financial-insecurity-a-
democratic-tilt-undercut-by-low-participation/

http://www.ers.usda.gov/topics/food-nutrition-assistance/food-security-in-the-
us.aspx

http://www.pbs.org/newshour/makingundisputed-facts-minimum-wage/-sense/

http://www.nytimes.com/2014/09/03/opinion/what-makes-people-poor.html

http://help.feedingAmerica.org/HungerInAmerica/FB161_NH_Manchester_repo
rt.pdf

https://www.gsfb.org/hunger/

http://www.fns.usda.gov/outreach/business-case-increasing-supplemental-
nutrition-assistance-program-snap-participation

https://www.nationalpriorities.org/budget-basics/federal-budget-101/spending/

http://www.nhfoodbank.org/Hunger-Study-2012.aspx

http://www.gsfb.org/wp-content/uploads/2014/10/FB259_report.pdf

news.illinois.edu/news/12/0531seniorhunger_CraigGundersen.html

http://www.theatlantic.com/business/archive/2014/10/the-top-1-percentand-01-
percentof-every-age-group-in-America/382094/

http://www.ted.com/talks/paul_piff_does_money_make_you_mean/transcript?la
nguage=en

http://www.nytimes.com/2014/08/08/opinion/paul-krugman-inequality-is-a-
drag.html?_r=0

http://www.heritage.org/research/reports/2014/12/federal-spending-by-the-
numbers-2014

http://www.hannaford.com/content.jsp?pageName=charitableFoundation&leftNa
vArea=AboutLeftNav

http://www.cnpp.usda.gov/sites/default/files/CostofFoodDec2014_0.pdf

http://frac.org/pdf/thrifty_food_plan_2012.pdf

http://www.maine.gov/dhhs/ofi/services/snap/faq.html

http://www.slate.com/blogs/moneybox/2015/04/13/adjunct_pay_a_quarter_of_
part_time_college_faculty_receive_public_assistance

http://www.salvationfarms.org/

http://www.rutlandfarmandfood.org/

http://www.getrealmaine.com/index.cfm/fuseaction/home.showpage/pageID/77/

http://www.maine.gov/dacf/ard/senior_farm_share.shtml

http://nhfoodbank.org/Grow-Local-Eat-Local.aspx

http://www.nhfoodbank.org/Individuals-and-Group-Opportunities.aspx

https://www.nokidhungry.org/pdfs/Facts-Childhood-Hunger-in-America-2013-grid.pdf

http://www.vermontfoodbankblog.com/2015/05/putney-foodshelf-family-food-bag-program.html?utm_source=Facebook&utm_mediu

https://carsey.unh.edu/publications?keyword=hunger&date[min][date]=&date[max][date]=2014

https://en.wikipedia.org/wiki/Social_class_in_the_United_States

https://en.wikipedia.org/wiki/New_Hampshire_locations_by_per_capita_income

http://www.ers.usda.gov/topics/food-nutrition-assistance/food-security-in-the-us/measurement.aspx

http://usatoday30.usatoday.com/news/health/2009-08-23-dialysis_N.htm

http://www.people-press.org/2015/01/08/the-politics-of-financial-insecurity-a-democratic-tilt-undercut-by-low-participation/

http://www.pbs.org/newshour/making-sense/undisputed-facts-minimum-wage/

http://www.nytimes.com/2014/09/03/opinion/what-makes-people-poor.html?_r=0

https://news.illinois.edu/blog/view/6367/205050

http://www.theatlantic.com/business/archive/2013/09/all-the-older-single-ladies-in-poverty/280036/

http://www.theatlantic.com/international/archive/2014/05/the-danger-of-financial-ignorance-do-you-understand-money/361851

ABOUT THE AUTHOR

Michele C Moore is a retired physician and the author of a number of non-fiction books, primarily health-related, and one book of poetry and short prose. She lives in New Hampshire and is on the board of a nearby food program.

www.ingramcontent.com/pod-product-compliance
Lightning Source LLC
Chambersburg PA
CBHW062144280526
45788CB00001B/303